5/14/84

Dear Hollis.

Thanks for everything.
I hope you enjoy this!

Best Wish

Ranl

PUTTING IT ON THE LINE

The Negotiating Secrets, Tactics, and Techniques of a Top Sports and Entertainment Agent

DAVID FISHOF and EUGENE SHAPIRO

With an Introduction by Brent Musburger

William Morrow and Company, Inc.

New York | 1983

Library of Congress Catalog Card Number: 83-62246

ISBN: 0-688-02447-5

Printed in the United States of America

First Edition

1 2 3 4 5 6 7 8 9 10

BOOK DESIGN BY VICTORIA HARTMAN

To Monica.
I couldn't be
where I am
without you.

PREFACE

I have come to learn one important lesson in all my years of representing professional athletes and show business celebrities: The winner is not necessarily the player with the best statistics or the celebrity with the biggest credit; the winner is the person who is able to negotiate the best contract. Being the best, having the most talent is not enough; you have to know how to translate your best into real dollars and cents.

In my seminars and lectures I constantly meet people from all walks of life, who are out there working very hard and getting very little for their efforts. You can change that for yourself. Aside from the entertaining glimpses into the world of sports and show business contract negotiations, this book is filled with tips, strategies, and step-by-step procedures that will allow you to translate your skills, time, and efforts into getting you what you deserve.

Many people don't even try to negotiate; they fear they have to be tough and unbending in order to win. That's not true! I enjoy my work, I love it, and if there is one message in this book, it is: Nice guys *can* finish first.

So, come along with me, sit by my side, watch and learn as I constantly put myself on the line and come out a winner.

ACKNOWLEDGMENTS

Over the years there have been many people who have given me guidance, trust, and precious time, especially my many clients without whom I would not have succeeded. To them I will always be grateful.

I especially want to thank: Betty Marks, Jerry Weiss, Art Raymond, Marvin Sears, Herschel Bernardi, Burgess Owens, Tom Illius, Stu Welz, Rob Heller, Bert Padell, Phil Citron, Ed Barton, Greg Mullins, Marty Klein, Van Harris, Ron Eliran, Ed Micone, Isabelle Giardino, Art Stolnitz, and my associate and friend Howie Silverman.

To Tam Mossman who had the original idea for this book and brought me and Eugene together; to my agent, Mel Berger of the William Morris Agency, who negotiated on my behalf; to my fellow comrade club-date bookers on 57th Street; to my editor, Nick Bakalar, who believed in my story and always kept me laughing.

Most important, I want to thank Sweet Lou, Big Vinnie, Hacksaw, jokester Phil, papa Jack, coach Bobby, Big Jetes and their lovely wives and children.

To my parents and Grandmother Rose, who have always backed me with their loving support, and to Eugene D. Shapiro who collaborated with me on this book, working in our homes, offices, coffee shops, health clubs, in between phone calls, and on the QE2, and whose friendship I will always treasure.

Contents

Introduction

A good agent is worth millions.

A bad agent can get you fired.

David Fishof's clients never lack work at a good price, which speaks well for his ability.

He shares a common characteristic with all successful ten-percenters. The man will call you twenty-four hours a day regardless of whether you're working, sleeping, loving, or daydreaming. Eventually, the George Steinbrenners and Georgia Frontieres have to say yes because the Fishof persistence simply wears them down.

In his book, Fishof takes you behind the scenes, where the important decisions are always made in the somewhat insulated world of sport.

You'll be intrigued by how Vince Ferragamo, a handsome quarterback with a strong arm, wound up playing in Montreal for a bankrupt team, and then returned to the Los Angeles Rams to play for an owner who'd sworn she would never take him back.

Ferragamo's success on the football field pales alongside Fishof's at the negotiating table, although David still laments how quickly Canadian entrepreneur Nelson Skalbania ran out of money. When you read the details of Ferragamo's multimillion-dollar contract, you'll understand why.

You will also get a close look at how George Steinbrenner negotiates for his New York Yankees. Fishof marched into Steinbrenner's office with Lou Piniella, an aging outfielder who would

13

probably get a pair of base hits in the middle of a Kansas tornado, but whose best days seemed to be behind him.

Steinbrenner offered a one-year contract. Piniella walked out with three years guaranteed, and The Boss even had kind words to say about Fishof.

Negotiating is a subtle art. Most entertainers and athletes aren't prepared to ask for what they're worth. That never bothered David Fishof. He always starts out by asking for more, and then gets you what you're worth. Nothing could be fairer—for both sides.

—BRENT MUSBURGER

PUTTING IT ON THE LINE

CHAPTER

1

KING GEORGE

George Steinbrenner has a reputation as a brash, aggressive, determined—some would say ruthless—businessman. One thing for sure, Steinbrenner is a businessman, always looking to turn his investments—in companies and in people—into profit. His approach—the end justifies the means—has worked for him; he has gotten a lot of press and media coverage, and has made a lot of money.

Steinbrenner comes off as a heavy. He loves the accolade; he enjoys being the center of attention. He relishes controversy.

How would I deal with Steinbrenner? That's what I was asking myself in November 1981 as I was standing in front of the offices of the American Ship Building Corporation in Tampa, Florida. Inside the building was Steinbrenner's office, and I had an appointment with him. Standing beside me was Lou Piniella, the New York Yankee right fielder. Lou wanted a new contract and I was Lou's agent. I had never met Steinbrenner, but I knew—or thought I knew—what to expect from him.

Steinbrenner's office surprised me. It looked like a doctor's reception room—Danish modern furniture (that's 1950's modern), spindly walnut legs on the chairs and sofas, worn foam-rubber cushions. There were several tables, again with those spindly legs and a bunch of old magazines on the tops. The walls were covered with photos of Steinbrenner's ships, huge ships. The first thing he wanted you to know when you walked into his office was that he owned big things.

17

We had arrived punctually at 10:30, our appointment time. We were told politely that Mr. Steinbrenner was not yet in. I half expected it. He would keep us waiting to show us who was boss. *Boss!* His employees called him THE BOSS. He was exactly that; what he wanted he got. He set out to do something and, with the arrogance of immense wealth, he usually got his way. Some people have accused Steinbrenner of being a spoiled kid who bullies everyone because he owns the ball, the bat, and even the ball field. He also happens to have a couple of World Series championships to prove he knows what he's doing.

Lou and I sat on a sofa, and Lou started talking to me. I picked up a magazine and suggested he do the same. "You never know who's listening; the walls have ears."

I leafed through the magazine, but didn't focus on anything in particular. I tried to get a feeling of the place, something that would tell me more about George Steinbrenner, more than I had heard and read. Everything in the room, in the air, confirmed my impressions; he was a man who took great joy in owning things—money, success, and people. He didn't care if what he owned was tacky or stylish. It was a question of the power of ownership. Everything was *his property*. He paid, he bought things—including loyalty. Lou Piniella owed loyalty, not to the Yankees but to George Steinbrenner personally. That's the way Steinbrenner would look at things. That would be the handle I would use to defuse him.

He finally arrived fifty minutes late. His face was set the minute he walked through the door, jaw squared, lips tight, a scowl on his brow. We shook hands; he had a powerful handshake. There was no apology for being so late. He wasn't late—he was doing what he wanted to do.

George Steinbrenner is a broad-shouldered, barrel-chested man, well dressed, oozing confidence. And with his broken hand in a cast and sling from a well-publicized altercation in Los Angeles—he was accosted in an elevator by two Dodgers fans and supposedly broke his hand in the process of laying both guys out—he looked even more ferocious. Here was a battler!

That macho aura didn't bother me. I'm a pretty big man myself, taller and heavier than Steinbrenner, but I knew I had to be careful. This man was a battleship. I couldn't bump him. He'd bump back, and he had bigger guns. Besides, I know you don't win by fighting with a man like him. I had no intention of fighting. Actually, I liked him. I liked him right away.

In any case, I wasn't there to battle, but to make sure Lou Piniella would get what he deserved. Lou and I met in 1977. I was a twenty-year-old kid booking shows into Catskills, New York, hotels and athletes into sports camps in the Northeast. I had arranged a personal appearance for Lou at Camp Ramaquois in Pomona, New York, and after I drove him home, he handed me a twenty-dollar bill. "For gas," he said, because he felt it wasn't my responsibility to get him to the job. It was my car, so he paid for the gas. He invited me into his house for lunch and we talked; and by the end of the meal we agreed that I would represent him, get him personal appearances and commercial endorsements. Since then, we've not only done business together, we've become friends and he's taught me a lot.

One night—it was in September 1981, six weeks after the demoralizing baseball players' strike, a month before the play-offs and the World Series—Lou called me at home. He just wanted to talk; he was feeling a little depressed. He wasn't having as good a year as usual. He was wondering if his career was over and speculating about the kinds of businesses he might want to get into.

"Do you think your career is over?" I asked him.

"Hmm, I don't know. Nah. I guess I really want to keep playing."

"Can you?"

"Yes."

"Then?"

"I just don't know. George . . . I got a feeling George won't give me another contract."

I heard the words, but I knew he wasn't ready to quit. It wasn't in his heart. Lou eats and sleeps the game. The first time he came into my office I noticed he couldn't sit in the chair for more than five minutes. He was edgy, and finally got up and practiced batting stances. Lou insisted I go to the game that night. "I'm gonna give you a bat for your office." Why he thought I needed a bat in the office wasn't quite clear at the time, but I found out later that we could talk for hours with me behind the desk and Lou standing up, swinging the bat as we talked business. His wife, Anita, told me he keeps a bat by his bed and practices before they go to bed.

I knew that more than anything else in the world, Lou wanted another contract from George Steinbrenner. He wanted to play two more years. At thirty-eight, he was sure he had it in him. He wanted to play till he was forty. It would be a milestone, and he wanted to end his career as a Yankee.

I told him not to worry; wait till after the Series. Lou was a money ballplayer. The Series was important not only to his future in baseball, but to his future in business. He would get a lot of media exposure. Everyone was certain the Yankees would be in the Series. I told Lou to wait before making any decision; wait and see what he did in the Series, see how he felt, see what was happening in the free-agent market, and, most important, see what Steinbrenner would do.

Lou had been a Yankee eight years. Steinbrenner had owned the team nine years. They had grown into being Yankees together. They had gained national recognition together as Yankees. Many fans, and Lou himself as well, believed there was a special bond between them. They both lived in Tampa, Florida. They were neighbors, *friends.* They had always negotiated Lou's contract between themselves. Just a deal between two buddies. Steinbrenner offered Lou a figure. Lou countered, and they settled somewhere in the middle. Lou was content with the money and the fact he had avoided a hassle with his friend. Steinbrenner was happy at saving himself a bundle.

There's an old negotiating tactic where an employee asks and deserves $40,000 and the employer says he can only afford between $28,000 and $30,000. The employee settles for $30,000 and thinks he's gotten the best of the deal.

Lou was outstanding in the Series. He always did well in crisis situations; that was part of his value. He delivered when it counted, even when he wasn't playing regularly. Fans respected him for it. They came to see him, hoping he'd get up to bat at a crucial moment and deliver.

Lou was worth a lot to the Yankees. Known for his humor when tension erupts in the clubhouse, he is an achiever and has five championship rings to prove it. That winning attitude was great for the younger players.

Lou was a favorite and drew attendance. Because of my experience in the entertainment business, where I cut deals based on attendance, I knew Lou translated into money in George Steinbrenner's pocket.

During the Series, Lou and I spoke daily so that I would have an insight into what was going on with the Yankees. He was buoyant, confident that he and Steinbrenner would get together and talk. I suggested he declare himself a free agent as soon as the Series was over. I wanted him to do it early so that other teams would know he was available. More important, I told Lou it was essential that Steinbrenner know that he meant business.

But Lou didn't want to declare. He was afraid Steinbrenner would get angry and then never offer him a new contract. He and Steinbrenner had worked it out before; they would do it again. There was nothing to worry about.

One phone call from Cedric Tallis, the Yankee vice-president for player operations, threw cold water on all this wishful thinking. Tallis offered Lou a one-year contract. When Lou asked for two, Tallis suggested he enter the free-agent market.

It hit Lou like a bombshell. He was stunned. *A phone call.* Lou couldn't believe it. He felt terrible, hurt, disappointed that Steinbrenner hadn't personally contacted him. Why hadn't he? They'd known each other for years. Why hadn't George talked to him, face-to-face like a man? Lou wasn't a kid. He understood age was against him, but he was sure he could overcome any of Steinbrenner's objections and get his two years.

That's why Steinbrenner hid. He didn't even want to give Lou a chance to make his case.

Lou kept making calls to Steinbrenner. The calls were never returned. He turned to me for advice. I asked Lou if he wanted me to negotiate for him.

"Yes," he answered.

I knew what Lou wanted and what he was worth in the market. "That means if I can get you a two-year contract at your worth on *any* team, I do it!"

This time Lou didn't answer so fast. He had a problem. On the one hand, he wanted to play for the Yankees. On the other hand, he wanted what he deserved. He knew if he declared free agency, he might get what he deserved, but then he'd no longer be a

Yankee, so certain was he that Steinbrenner would not even talk to him if he declared. Lou Piniella's greatest concern was Steinbrenner's reaction.

My experience has been that owners and general managers always tell their athletes, "I'll take care of you." George Steinbrenner had always said it to Lou, and now Steinbrenner wouldn't even talk to him on the phone.

"Okay," Lou said finally. It sounded as if someone were squeezing the words out of him. "I really want to play two years." Then he added in a very determined voice, "But David, I really want to play them as a Yankee."

"You leave that to me."

However, Lou didn't listen to me. He just couldn't understand why George hadn't given him a contract, why they hadn't reached an agreement as they had in the past. He kept trying to reach George. He also kept delaying declaring himself a free agent, for fear that it would destroy any chance he might have of remaining a Yankee.

A story by Henry Hecht in the *New York Post* changed the situation radically. Hecht wrote that Lou Piniella must mean business because he hired David Fishof to represent him in his negotiations with Steinbrenner, or with other owners if he declared himself a free agent.

This piece of news brought yet another phone call from Tallis. Only this time Tallis suggested that Lou call George.

"I've been trying for some time," Lou said, holding back his anger.

"Try him now" was Tallis's advice.

Sure enough, Steinbrenner was available and talking. He offered Lou a one-year contract at his 1981 salary—$300,000.

Lou felt Steinbrenner hadn't treated him fairly; how often he had called with the only response a suggestion from the front office that he become a free agent. "It was you who told me to declare as a free agent."

Steinbrenner didn't answer Lou's accusation. All he said was "Lou, I want you to play for the Yankees. You gonna take my offer?"

"Let me think about it. I'll call you."

Lou was on the phone to me immediately. He told me what

had happened. He had seen Steinbrenner do his number on Sparky Lyle, Billy Martin, and Reggie Jackson, on everyone. Now he was doing it on him. Lou was hurt and angry and wanted Steinbrenner to know it.

I believed that Lou, being the kind of money player he is, could get a job with any ball club. But was that what he wanted? I didn't think so. I could feel his Latin temperament getting the best of him. I told him not to take this personally. After all, pro sports is a business.

"Okay. Then I won't take it personally. I don't want to be a Yankee. Go out and get me the best deal you can get."

Then and there I got a commitment from Lou. He would do nothing rash. He would sign nothing, say nothing, do nothing until I advised him.

Time was our big problem. The rules state that a free agent or his representative can contact teams between the time he declares free agency and the draft, but only to discuss what he is looking for in length of contract and to determine if a team is interested. Normally all discussions have to stop three days before the draft but because of the strike, an agreement was reached that contacts could be made right up to the day of the draft.

Here it was Sunday, November 8. The draft was the following Friday, the thirteenth. We had only four working days. Four days to find out who wanted him. Not that I expected him to play on any other team—in fact, there was no question in my mind that Lou would be a Yankee. It was just a matter of getting what he wanted and what he deserved. Steinbrenner had made a legitimate offer. Where there's a real offer, there's interest; and it was my job now to turn that interest around and hook Steinbrenner on it.

I had to find out who else wanted Lou; it would tell me his worth. It would tell me the kind of leverage I would have when I sat down to negotiate a contract with Steinbrenner.

Logistics was another problem. I got Lou's call just before I was leaving for the airport. I had to be in Los Angeles for several days, and the meetings I had the following day, Monday, could not be postponed. When I got to the airport, I called Lou and told him to get back to Steinbrenner and set up a meeting during the week. It could be anywhere, any day except Monday. It couldn't be Friday either; that was the day of the draft. I told him where I was staying in L.A., and to get word to me as soon as possible.

When I got to the Beverly Hilton Hotel, there was a message waiting for me. The meeting was set for Wednesday, 10:30 in the morning, in Tampa.

I called Lou and told him to get in touch with Marvin Miller (the head of the Baseball Players Association) and declare himself a free agent. Do it first thing in the morning. And to be sure it got into the papers.

He argued against doing that. "We've got a meeting with George. Why get him angry?"

"Lou, try it my way," I said.

I felt we needed to show strength. A man like George Steinbrenner likes to go up against strength. He sees it as a challenge. With Reggie Jackson, Bobby Murcer, and Ron Guidry all free agents, and Guidry's agent annihilating Steinbrenner in the newspapers and Reggie not being his favorite, I felt that Steinbrenner needed to show the fans he wasn't deserting them by letting his players go. And Lou had strength because of the time element; Steinbrenner would want to sign one guy before the draft.

I had one full day to get something that would give me leverage with Steinbrenner. At least I had a couple of hours' headstart against the sun. I got up while it was still dark in Los Angeles and started calling back east.

Lou and I had already reviewed the teams, those he wouldn't mind playing for, and the parks he hit well in, plus the cities he could live in.

The first person I spoke to was Haywood Sullivan, president of the Boston Red Sox. Piniella had a name in Boston. The Red Sox' remember how Lou robbed them of a title in the '78 playoffs with a fantastic catch in the setting sun. They also knew his stats in Fenway.

At first Sullivan didn't believe me. He hadn't heard that Piniella had declared free agency. When a player declares himself a free agent, a cable is sent from the Baseball Players Association to every team in major-league baseball. It was 9:30 A.M. on the East Coast, Sullivan hadn't received any cable. Who knew if it had even been sent yet?

I told Sullivan Lou had declared and the cable was on its way, but he was reluctant to talk to me. No matter what I said, he still didn't believe Lou Piniella would declare free agency. And besides, he added, he was looking for youth to build a ball club. He already had his token old men; Tony Perez and Carl Yastrzemski.

Next, Houston. By this time, the cable was beginning to catch up with my calls. Steinbrenner and the Astros had been at odds for some time. Al Rosen was the general manager at Houston. Steinbrenner had treated Rosen shabbily when he was president of the Yankees. I figured Rosen would jump at the chance to get back at Steinbrenner. Unfortunately, that kind of revenge was too expensive and Rosen passed it by.

I went to my meetings in L.A., and instead of eating lunch, I made more calls. Several people were out and would call back. But then I got Buzzie Bavasi, vice-president of the California Angels, and got all the information I needed.

Bavasi and I had met at the Los Angeles office of our mutual attorney, Marvin Sears, the guiding genius in a Century City law firm. At that time I was in the process of pulling the plug out of the Los Angeles Rams' hopes of going back to the Super Bowl (see Chapter 4). Bavasi knew who I was and took the call.

He was sympathetic. He understood what Lou wanted, why he wanted it, and that Lou was a ballplayer worth having on the team. But there was nothing Bavasi could do. "Look," he said. "I like Piniella. Always have. But he's never going to leave George. More important, *George will never let him go.*"

"That's not true," I said quickly.

"No?"

"He'll leave. He wants to play ball two more years. He doesn't care where he plays as long as he gets a chance to play and can help a team. He can help the Angels."

I heard what sounded like a snicker at the other end of the phone. "David," Bavasi said, "it doesn't matter what Lou wants. It's up to George. Last week we had an owners' meeting in Tempe, Arizona."

"Yeah."

"You know? Do you also know what George said at that meeting?"

"About what?"

"George got up and said . . . well, I don't remember the exact words, but in effect he said that whoever offers Guidry one million, he'll go one point one, and he'll keep on going. You know George. It wasn't a quiet statement. It was a *challenge*.

"You know how much money George has to throw around?" Bavasi went on. "I wouldn't go after a player he liked or wanted . . . and let me tell you something, David, he likes Lou Piniella."

That was exactly what I wanted to hear, and everything seemed to be falling into place. But by the time I got to the airport, it looked like I wouldn't even make the meeting. My flight to Tampa, via Atlanta, was canceled—a bomb scare. The flight was going to be delayed several hours. I would miss the Atlanta connection and wind up in Tampa Wednesday afternoon, hours too late.

I found a plane going to Miami. If I was lucky I would catch a connecting flight to Tampa, getting there early in the morning.

On the plane I went over all the facts and figures on Lou. I always write everything down to be prepared. I went through the options—hell, there were no options. I didn't need any. The option of going free agent had already paid off. It had gotten Steinbrenner's interest and given me the kind of information I needed.

My plane landed early in Miami. I'd have no trouble making the connecting flight to Tampa. In fact, I had almost an hour; so I rushed to the men's room, washed my hair in the sink, shaved with an electric razor, and put on a clean shirt. Now I was ready to face George Steinbrenner.

I got to Tampa a little after 9:00 and took a cab to an address Lou had given me. The place was a greasy spoon across the street from Steinbrenner's office. Lou ate. I didn't. I just sat. I never eat before a negotiation. I don't want to be satisfied, think or feel satisfied, when I walk into such a meeting. I walk in hungry and expect to walk out satisfied.

Lou and I talked. I had to be sure he would allow me to negotiate. He had never used an agent before with Steinbrenner. It would be a totally new experience for him, and I couldn't have him butting in when he had gotten what he wanted and thought it was over. It had to be what I wanted, what I knew he deserved. I made him understand we were going into a negotiation—it was an employer-employee relationship, and he should forget that George Steinbrenner was his friend. For the next hour or two, it was business, my business, and he was to keep out of it.

I asked Lou what he wanted.

"Six hundred thousand for two years. That's my bottom line, David. If you can get that, let's sign and run."

He wanted those two years, *guaranteed*, no matter what.

Lou is a smart businessman. He knows his value as a player and as a name, but negotiating with someone he's been involved with is another matter. There were a lot of personal ties between Lou and Steinbrenner that would get in the way, and it was my role to make sure that didn't happen. We had agreed that I would do the talking about contracts and that he would discuss only baseball.

Now finally we were ready to do business. Steinbrenner led us into his office, but Lou stopped before entering to chat with one of George's executives. I found myself in the room alone with Steinbrenner. The walls, as in the reception room, were covered with pictures of his ships, but here they were not alone. Yankee memorabilia were scattered around. He had decorated the room to show his power, the things he owned.

But it was the desk that blew my mind. Certainly I expected a large desk, something he could use to impress and intimidate. But this was the craziest and most obvious *club* I had ever seen in negotiations. One part of the desk was sickle shaped, a six-foot-long arching curve about three feet wide. And coming out from the center was a ten-foot extension. It looked like . . . well, you can guess what it looked like.

Steinbrenner sat behind his desk and invited me to sit in a chair at the end of the desk extension—he at one end, me at the other. Was he trying to impress me or shoot me?

Instead, I took the chair that had been carefully placed for me and moved it around to the side so that I was across the desk from Steinbrenner a little off to the left. Now he had to turn to talk to me.

Steinbrenner knew who I was. He knew the kind of contract I had secured from the Montreal Alouettes for Vince Ferragamo. Cedric Tallis had known Nelson Skalbania, the new owner of the

Alouettes, when Skalbania had a triple-A baseball club. The word had gotten out; the contract had set a precedent. It was the first deal where a ballplayer got a major percentage of the gate. For an owner that was a terrible sword, which could cut anywhere.

We started with chitchat—the weather, the flight from L.A. I have a theory: everyone has two businesses, his own and show business. Everyone either is involved in some aspect of show business or is attached to it vicariously.

I have booked and am very friendly with the singer and female impersonator Marilyn Michaels, who had been in the road company of *Funny Girl*. I knew Steinbrenner had invested in the show. We talked about *Funny Girl*, what he had invested, what he had made.

"What did you think of Billy Joel?" I asked him.

"Billy Joel?" Steinbrenner's eyes opened a little.

I had known Billy Joel for some time. Billy was a Yankee fanatic, and even though a name entertainer, he had never met a Yankee in the flesh. I set up a dinner at Billy Joel's house for Lou Piniella, Bobby Murcer, and me, along with our wives. Everyone got along terrifically. Lou invited Billy Joel to a game and to come meet the players in the dugout. Steinbrenner had loved the publicity, and now he suddenly understood who had made the connection. Lou came into the room at this point and moved a chair in behind me; he had cleverly waited exactly the right amount of time. Steinbrenner and I now had developed a rapport.

"What are you here for?" George asked as he came forward in his chair. For a minute I thought he was going to leap across the desk at me.

"We're here to discuss a long-term contract."

"Things are going to be different on the Yankees this year." He still hadn't gotten over the Yankee loss in the Series. "We're going for youth and speed. Lou's thirty-nine." He snapped his words out at me. So this was the famous Steinbrenner bark. But I also knew there was bite behind that bark. His eyes were staring straight at me and they were as cold as the steel hulls of his ships.

"Lou's only thirty-eight and he also hit .457 in the play-offs. Best on any team. He's the only one, the only one," I repeated for emphasis, "who came through when it counted."

"That was last year." Steinbrenner waved a hand in the air as if to dismiss the memory. He sat back in his chair. "Lou will be a year older. A year's a long time when you're thirty-eight."

"So at least we agree Lou's thirty-eight." I smiled.

Steinbrenner smiled.

I ran down the ballplayers who were older than Lou and were still contributing. "Forget the older ones," I said when their names were getting no response. "What about the million-dollar player you have who didn't deliver in the World Series?"

"He apologized to me," Steinbrenner said by way of rebuttal and quickly changed the subject. He asked Lou what he thought of Charlie Lau.

Lou jumped up immediately. He had been imprisoned in his chair for almost forty-five minutes. I was surprised he'd been able to sit still so long and not say anything. He saw his chance with Steinbrenner's question.

He pretended he had a bat in his hands and took up a batting stance—one of Charlie Lau's. "Charlie keeps telling you to put out the left shoulder," Lou said as he patted his left shoulder to get it to stick farther out.

"I disagree. Now, this is my batting stance," Lou went on, digging his shoes into the carpet and pulling his left shoulder back. "Here's the difference between my batting stance and Charlie Lau's."

Steinbrenner said nothing.

Lou sat down and I turned to Steinbrenner. "Let's structure the deal like a football contract." I knew Steinbrenner was a football buff. "Remember Griese? What was the slogan of the GM's [general managers] of the NFL? 'First you put in your years of duty, then we'll pay you.' Bob Griese was the highest-paid player in the NFL his last year and hardly played one down."

Steinbrenner turned to Lou and said, "It's about time you got yourself an agent."

That was my cue. "As an agent, George, I'm here to get Lou what he deserves. A good contract not only for Lou Piniella, but good for the Yankees. A contract that we will not only be proud of, but one people will say George Steinbrenner can be proud of."

Steinbrenner was used to flattery. He knew I was flattering

him; he liked it. His face relaxed. "Okay. I think Lou has one more year in him. I want him to play that year for the Yankees. He can have a year."

"Lou has two good years in him, George."

Steinbrenner turned to Lou. "That's why I recommended you become a free agent. I can't use you for two years. Maybe some other club can." Steinbrenner's voice was soothing, like a father giving his son advice.

I could feel Lou's hot breath behind me.

"George, if we have to go the free-agent route, I'll have to go public about Lou disliking the Yankees and you."

"Me?"

"I got to convince the other clubs that Lou's serious, that he's not in the free-agent draft as a bargaining position with George Steinbrenner. Lou doesn't want to do it. He doesn't really want to be a free agent and besides"—I had to bring him back to where he was the boss—"how free is Lou? Everyone knows you got up at the owners' meeting last week and said if anyone offers Guidry a million, you'd go one point one. How free is Guidry?"

He stuttered a little. "No, no. That's not what I said at the meeting."

I had to keep him remembering what he'd said, and especially why he'd said it—his possessiveness. They were his ballplayers. It was his ball, his bat, his park. Nobody was going to take his players away from him.

"How free is Lou really, George? I've talked to people. Lou's wanted out there. But people are reluctant because of your friendship with him. People understand that and respect that. Remember Burger King?"

Burger King had done a set of Yankee baseball cards for a promotion. Lou's photo had been left out inadvertently. It was Steinbrenner's son who had brought it to his father's attention. As soon as Steinbrenner found out, he immediately ordered a reprinting that included Piniella.

"Do you know why people are *afraid* to even try to take Lou away from you? They don't believe you'll ever let him go. They see you and Lou as two men who have made it as Yankees. Both of you started from scratch and brought pride back to the Yankees. Lou as a player, you as the man who rebuilt the team. You brought them back into the winners' circle after they'd been out for a long time. You restored their pride, what it meant to be a Yankee, a winner! Lou Piniella is part of that. You lose Lou Piniella, George, you lose a piece of the Yankees."

George Steinbrenner sat in his chair, relaxed, confident, assured. His face was dead serious. He believed every word I said. He believed it because I had spoken with confidence. This was not flattery; I was absolutely sincere.

"Look, George, besides a playing contract, Lou wants to be part of the Yankee organization. He wants something he can do for the Yankees when his playing days are over." Steinbrenner didn't say a word, so I went right on laying out the terms of a contract.

We got down to business. We started with small details, like Lou's weight—which turned out not to be such a small matter—and worked our way up.

"As for the length of the contract, George . . ." I never got to finish the sentence.

"I want Lou for three years."

I heard a gasp from behind me. Lou knew he had just gotten his two years, *guaranteed.* "Three years, George?" I understood. He offered one. We wanted two. The only way to stay in control was to offer three. How could we turn that down? "But you know Lou only wants to play for two years."

"Okay. He plays for two years and the third he does public relations for the Yankees."

"Now the numbers, George." I had come with three proposals: $1 million, $1.3 million, $1.6 million. But these were numbers for two years. "What's your offer?"

Steinbrenner took a pen and jotted the numbers on a piece of paper and handed it to me. The numbers were $350,000 for the first year, $375,000 for the second year, and $400,000 for the third year.

One million one hundred twenty-five thousand dollars. I had been determined to get Lou double what he wanted. Just an hour and a half ago in the coffee shop, Lou had said he wanted $600,000 for two years. We were getting more than that on a three-year deal. I thought about it. I could have pressed Steinbrenner for another $100,000. But I wanted this to be a situation where everybody won. Lou would be able to live in harmony with Steinbrenner for the rest of his playing days, and Steinbrenner would leave Lou alone for the rest of his years.

I looked over at Lou for agreement. He got up and said, "Okay." I said, "Okay," and we all had a deal.

I want to look at the Piniella-Steinbrenner negotiation from three perspectives: first, what psychological factors were keeping Lou from getting what he deserved; second, how we had to establish his worth; third, what strategy had to be employed in dealing with a man like George Steinbrenner.

Psychological Factors

Translate What You Do into Dollars

Lou's essential problem was no different than that of millions of people. You work hard, you deliver for someone, and you don't get what you deserve.

Over the years Lou had made a lot of great plays, but he never translated those plays into money. Since he's an athlete first, his first thought is about his ability. He makes a great play; he says, "I have great ability." But a great play doesn't only indicate ability, it translates into money, and the money should be equal to the ability.

Most bosses pay compliments on your ability. "Great play!" they say, or "Good job," or "I see you made the deadline," or "Thanks for working overtime." It costs them nothing to say these things and, of course, it's nice to get compliments. But it's nicer to get paid for what you've done.

Translate every great play you make into money. Keep a record. A ballplayer gets paid on the basis of his statistics. What are your statistics—the time you've put in, the money you've saved the company, the innovations you've developed over a year? A boss forgets a lot, but if you have your statistics in front of him, he can't deny your claim. Don't rely on him to remember. Why should he? Show him what you've done.

And translate it when you make the great plays. When you produce, you should get what you deserve. In our economy you get paid as long as you deliver, but make sure to get the money *when* you deliver.

Standing up for Yourself

Another problem most people have is not wanting to rock the boat, so they accept what they're offered and don't stand up and ask for what they deserve. They're afraid that if they stand up, they'll get pushed overboard.

Lou had always negotiated with Steinbrenner under a "I-won't-rock-the-boat" mentality. He had always accepted Steinbrenner's offers. Now things were different; Steinbrenner wasn't offering. Lou was lucky in a way. He was being forced to stand up, to declare himself a free agent. It's quite possible that if he hadn't met the test, he might still have gotten a contract from Steinbrenner, but it would have been on Steinbrenner's terms. And Lou would have had to go through the whole process the following year, if there was a following year.

Many people fall into the "let's-not-rock-the-boat" trap. They're afraid to stand up for what they truly deserve. By not standing up, you get less, and the nagging fact that you got less makes you miserable. You say out loud you're mad at your boss, but the real anger is with yourself—and it's very difficult to admit it. So the anger grows inside, your job becomes miserable, and everything starts to sour.

Self-destructive Impulses

There is a great amount of self-destructiveness in many individuals. Lou never wanted to face a negotiating session with George Steinbrenner. Very few people look forward to a tough encounter, especially with someone who is supposed to be a "friend." Most people would rather not deal with such a situation. However, there they are, and they imagine that the easiest way to cope—although I believe it is the worst—is to try to get it over with as quickly as possible. Once you've done something about it, you say to yourself, "It's over, I can forget about it."

You're only fooling yourself. Of course, you can't forget about getting youself a bum deal. You have to live with what you've agreed to. In general people take less than they deserve and pay more than they should because they'd rather not negotiate.

Being Hasty Can Be a Risk

Most people make quick decisions. Most people don't want to hassle. They rationalize: "It was a spur-of-the-moment thing." Nonsense! They just didn't want to do the necessary homework, then carefully and systematically negotiate. They didn't want to say *here's what I deserve and here's why I deserve it.*

Whenever you make a quick decision, you're going to get beat. For years, Lou didn't want to negotiate, so he made quick decisions to get it over with, and, in my opinion, he got beat. Sure, he was making good money, but he could have been making more, much more.

It's the same rule no matter what you're negotiating for—a job, a raise, or merchandise. Look at all the frantic commercials on TV, with everyone running all over the place. They want you to think you have to decide fast, buy before it's too late. Decide today! They want you to think that if you don't get it today, you'll miss the chance of a lifetime.

But think about it. If the product or the job offer or whatever is that worthwhile, you can—you must—wait a day or two. You can test the market, get your information together, think it over, decide whether it is for you, and *then* go in and negotiate for it.

Fear as a Tactic

People like Steinbrenner thrive on causing fear. Steinbrenner always creates an aura of terror around him; he does it very effectively by firing and hiring managers, and by trading ballplayers like a kid trades baseball cards.

Steinbrenner instills fear for a reason: He wants to be sure the people he's dealing with are always unsure as to what he will do next. That keeps them worrying and off guard. Instead of doing what they should be doing, or concentrating on getting what they need, they have to look constantly over their shoulders to see what Steinbrenner is doing and how he will react to what *they're* doing. By instilling this kind of fear, Steinbrenner has been able to change the emphasis from what others need to what he wants.

Instead of Lou setting out a proposal for himself that he could live with, he was trying to create one that Steinbrenner could live with.

The lesson to be learned is quite simple. Do what you have to do for yourself. Don't second-guess or look over your shoulder at someone's possible reaction. If you're conscientious about your decision, if you've made it with all the facts considered, it has to be the right decision for you and *beneficial to all those around you*.

Showing Your Strength

The obvious solution to fear is strength. What happens normally is that your opponent is so concerned about instilling fear that it becomes palpable and you react to it. You accept the fact that he is trying to make you afraid. You accept his rules for how the negotiations will be held, and you become defensive.

Don't give in to the fear your opponent wants to instill in you! Fight it with strength. Stand up and tell him what you want and why you deserve it. That usually works. Most bosses are not prepared for that kind of talk. They expect you to come in on your hands and knees.

In general, the fear tactic is used by people who consider themselves strong types. They instill fear, or try to, because they are so rarely challenged. They've gotten away with it so many times that it's become second nature to them. However, most of the strong types—Steinbrenner included—actually react very favorably to a show of strength, certainly more favorably than if you come trembling in. If you show your strength to someone like this, he's going to respond by deeming you a *worthwhile* opponent, someone he can respect. The very fact that you are prepared to stand up and go head-to-head will get you what you want. Your strength will appeal to him and you'll be able to make a deal.

Position

One of the biggest mistakes most people make in dealing with bosses, or with someone who holds a "higher" position, is that they allow the position to frighten them. The vice-president for personnel may sound like a powerful title, but don't let it scare you. Think of yourself as the president of your own personnel department. Elevate yourself to a position equal to your opponent's. Remember, if you didn't have something he wants, he wouldn't be talking with you. So as long as you're talking, keep remembering this is business, and people in business like to deal with people on the same level. Put yourself there.

Establishing Your Worth

Lou thought his worth was what he was willing to settle for. He based that assessment on what he had been paid in the past. His salary had established his worth. But that wasn't a true indication of his real worth. Lou would have taken $300,000 a year on a two-year contract, accepting the lower salary in exchange for the guaranteed two years. In effect, he would have accepted his worth as set by George Steinbrenner.

It's the same with most people. You don't know what you're worth if only your boss tells you. Why accept his evaluation? What's his prime concern? Your worth, or saving the company money? There's no reason for him to offer you more. Most of the time you'll accept the offer, so why should he stretch his budget?

We live in a free-market society; therefore, to establish your worth you have to test the market. With Lou, I had to go to other teams. I had to go to the competition. Other teams had scouted him. They knew what he had done. In many instances, it's the competition who knows your true value. The Toronto Blue Jays and three other American League teams had called Lou at home the night before we went to see Steinbrenner.

I know a man who was working as an accountant with a large accounting firm. He enjoyed his work and felt very happy in his office surroundings. Only, he had a problem: He was unhappy with his salary. He was earning $17,000 a year and thought he deserved more. He was coming up for a salary review and didn't know how to prove his worth in order to get what he deserved.

I suggested he go out and test the market. He did. He used his lunch hour. He answered ads in the papers; he took a day off and went for interviews. He was offered several jobs, one featuring as much as $35,000, plus a car. I told him to take it. The job would bring him up to his real worth, but he liked his old job and wanted to keep it; he just wanted a raise.

Now he knew what he was worth. When his salary review came up, he told his boss he would like to stay with the firm, but that he'd had offers from other firms that he had to consider seriously. He listed the offers, and showed his boss in black and white what he was worth. Because he'd gone out and established his value, he didn't have to whine or plead. He was secure in what he was asking for, and that gave him the power to negotiate. All of that came through, and his boss agreed with his evaluation of himself. They worked out a deal. He got an immediate raise to $25,000 with planned increments and the use of a company car.

When you know what you are worth, your boss will be a lot more amenable to your suggestions.

Negotiating Strategy

Guilt

Guilt was a very serious factor in the negotiations with Steinbrenner. He had not called Lou in to tell him to his face that he should become a free agent, someone else had called to do his bidding. I read this as Steinbrenner hiding. Why? I believed Steinbrenner had done—or wanted to do—something he himself thought was wrong. He felt guilty, and I was able to use that guilt when I talked about him and Lou and the Yankees, tying them all together into one package. To dump Lou was to dump the Yankees; to dump the Yankees was to dump himself.

Publicity

I had to look not just at how Steinbrenner acted toward Lou, but also consider what he thinks of himself. He sees himself as a winner, as much a superstar with the Yankees as any ballplayer, maybe more so. He wants to stay in the headlines, up front. Remember, Lou is a very popular player with the fans. His sounding off in this case would have been heard loud and clear. I'm sure

Steinbrenner read the possibility of Lou going public as a blow to his ego certainly, but he must also have been carefully considering how it would affect attendance and thus his income.

Eating

The comment about eating is as simple as it sounds. You eat, you are satisfied. Not only that, with food in your belly, the blood rushes to your stomach. That's not where you want it when you negotiate. You want it running through your head so that the oxygen keeps your head clear. Keep your stomach empty and your head full.

Power Plays and Power Symbols

Even before we met, Steinbrenner tried to make a power play by arriving late. He was showing *he* was the boss. But why come late? What did he gain? He actually ran the risk of alienating us. What kind of a negotiation session would we have had then?

I always wait a reasonable amount of time, but never more than an hour. I understand how easy it is to get hung up; people are doing business and things do suddenly crop up. But after an hour I leave. Remember, if they don't have the time for you now, they won't have the time for you later. You must have your own sense of self. Stand up and leave if you are kept waiting too long. If you have something the other side wants, they'll come after you. If they don't, then you know they weren't worth waiting for.

And take Steinbrenner's desk! Its size was supposed to affect anybody who had to sit in front of it.

Don't let the power symbols affect you. Steinbrenner didn't *need* to come late to prove that he could do what he wanted. He didn't need the oversized desk to prove what a big man he is. And you don't have to accept someone else's symbols for what *they* say they are. You're not dealing with lateness or a desk; you're there to deal with an issue.

There was a chair waiting for me. It was placed strategically for Steinbrenner's purposes. I simply moved it. He wanted me to sit in one place, where he thought he would have a physical advantage. I sat in another place. By doing this I not only denied him the power he saw in the symbol, but disrupted his setup. Rather than me facing him, he now had to face me.

If you walk into a room that has been set up to be intimidating, rearrange it. Say you can't sit in a soft chair. Say the light is in your eyes and move the chair. Say you have a bad neck; when you move it to the left you get pains, so you have to sit on the other side, etc. Shake up your opponent's power plays by using the very symbols he has set up to intimidate you.

Telling Lies

There are substantive lies and procedural lies. What I suggested about moving the chairs, or giving an excuse for moving, might be considered to be a lie. I see this as a procedural maneuver. However, I am dead set against substantive lies.

People do lie. Some of the lying is done intentionally, some by mistake, some as a natural way of negotiation. I caught Steinbrenner in a lie when he denied what he had said at the owners' meeting. This was a substantive lie. It dealt directly with the issue of whether Lou was "truly" a free agent or not; it dealt with whether Steinbrenner was really going to allow anyone to bid for Piniella.

Catching your opponent in a lie is a wonderful weapon that has been put in your hands. It's also a dangerous one, and you have to be careful how you use it. You don't want to insult him by accusing him of lying. After all, you're not there to judge your opponent; you're there to get what you came for. (This issue is very important and I'll talk more about it in Chapter 7.)

I did not accuse Steinbrenner of lying. I merely let him know I knew what was said at the meeting. He knew I knew not only what he had said but the intent behind it. Now he was out to correct the lie, and the only way he could do that was by agreeing that Lou had value to other teams, and therefore was worth something more than Steinbrenner was claiming for the Yankees.

Keeping to the Issue

In negotiations keep remembering why you're there. Keep focused on the issue. Don't go off on too many tangents. You're there for a purpose; stick to it. You don't want to be diverted, nor, you should assume, does your opponent.

It's okay to have a slight change of pace once in a while, like when Lou and Steinbrenner discussed batting, or when Steinbrenner and I discussed show business. But then you have to get back to the subject. Let your opponent know you know what's going on and what's at stake.

Assume the person you are dealing with is a busy person; his time is valuable. He doesn't want to sit around and chew the fat. If you do he'll think you have nothing else to do. It means your time isn't valuable, and if it isn't, then he'll be less likely to regard your negotiations as important.

Establishing Common Ground

All the talk about batting and show business was not beside the point in this case. It was a way to communicate something both sides were interested in *besides* the issues in the negotiations. Conversations of this nature should be looked upon as building bridges to common ground, to gain mutual respect. That's very important. Had we gone into a full discussion of batting or Broadway, it would have been a mistake. Once we had common ground, the subject was brought around to why we were there.

One last thing to learn from the negotiations. Don't be greedy. I might have gotten more money, but would it have been worth it? Always remember the straw that broke the camel's back. As soon as we received over a million dollars, Lou had gotten what he wanted, what he deserved—that's why we had come to negotiate.

CHAPTER

2

HOLLYWOOD

The phones are forever ringing at my home and in my office. A client wants advice, the Sands Hotel in Vegas wants The Mamas and the Papas, Resorts International in Atlantic City wants Gary Puckett, or Harrah's in Tahoe wants The Association. *Good Morning America* wants Lou Piniella, Isuzu Motors wants Jack Reynolds for a commercial, *Vogue* wants Phil Simms for a modeling session. Sometimes I find myself cradling two phones, talking to my secretary, and waving someone into the office—all at the same time. But spending time on the phone is a given in my business. The phone and I are inseparable.

One day I got a call from Fred Dryer, who had heard about me. The call came right before the Los Angeles Rams were about to play Pittsburgh in Super Bowl XIV.

Fred Dryer, one of the great defensive ends in the National Football League (NFL), has been at it since 1970. In 1981 when he called me, he was still considered one of the greats, still up on top, but he knew it was time to begin looking for a new career. Fred wanted to be an actor.

I was going to the Coast for the Super Bowl, so he and I agreed to meet and have dinner at R. J.'s in Beverly Hills the Thursday evening before the game.

Fred is a bit of an enigma. At six feet six inches and 231 pounds, he's one of the lightest players at his position. On the field he's like a cobra ready to strike. Quick, decisive, Fred is able to move

41

all his energy to a focal point within himself, hold it, and wait for the instant to move.

But if you spend time with him, you wonder how he ever moves so fast. Out of a football uniform, Fred is an analyzer; he's always thinking, pondering, being cautious. His face is always going, mouth moving up and down or sideways, his teeth biting one side of his lips and then the other. Like a meat grinder, his face takes in every word you say, weighs it carefully, munches it, digests it to get from it everything he can. With every word *he* speaks, it's the same process.

R. J.'s was Fred's choice for the meeting. It was a natural place to go, because he's something of a health nut, always walking around eating dates or a carrot or offering to share a piece of celery. He claims that oats and vegetables are his secret to success. Very few guys share his oats or vegetables—but then again, very few people laugh at him for eating them.

Dryer is a bit of a Jack Kerouac character—but without the booze and drugs. Before he bought a home in Long Beach, he lived in a truck for years—a VW van with a bed in it. When he finally stopped playing football and started acting, he lived at Bob Stenner's house. Stenner's a CBS producer whose specialty is sports: the Super Bowl, shows like *NBA Challenge*, NFL football on the weekends.

Stenner has a beautiful four-bedroom house in the San Fernando Valley. An old friend of Fred's, Stenner invited him to make full use of the house so he wouldn't have to commute from Burbank to Long Beach every day while putting his show business career together. Fred accepted the offer but didn't live in Stenner's house. He parked his van in the driveway and lived in the van! Whenever I called Fred, Stenner had to go out to his driveway, knock on the van, and get him.

But now we were sitting in R. J.'s three days before the Super Bowl and Fred was talking about changing careers.

"I got a great contract now," he said slowly, drawing out the words one at a time. "A no-cut clause." (A no-cut-clause contract is hard to get in the NFL, but Fred had managed it by negotiating directly with Carroll Rosenbloom; he took less money to remain in Los Angeles instead of going to New Orleans.) "Mine's one of the few in the league," he went on, "but I only have a few good years left."

He looked at me, his face serious, his eyes searching mine for a reading. But my face was deadpan—no expression. I was listening.

He took a bite of his salad. I swear he must have chewed the lettuce and tomato for five minutes before he spoke again: "It's time I looked around at what I'm going to do with the rest of my life."

I was honestly impressed. The Rams were finally in the Super Bowl, and Fred had helped them get there. The city was crazy with Super Bowl fever. People—including celebrities—were sending drinks to us, coming by to say hello, and wishing Dryer luck. And all the while he was talking about what he was going to do with the rest of his life. That kind of thinking and planning is what makes him so great at playing football and, perhaps, at anything else he concentrates on.

"Look," he said, biting the right side of his lower lip, "too many athletes expect to go into acting and become stars overnight because they've got names. Maybe they get put into a picture or two and then they're out the back door. It's like football." Again he looked straight at me to see if I was listening. "You gotta deliver what the competition is delivering. Once the sports notoriety wears off, you gotta know how to *act*. You gotta stand on your own merits." He was smart enough and sensitive enough to know the adulations and offers come in only as long as you're winning, as long as you're good. But no one stays great in sports forever. Once those heady celebrity days passed, he knew the fans, the promoters, the movie producers would soon forget about him. He wanted to ensure his future by starting on the right foot *now* while he had an advantage.

I had already made up my mind about him, but I had to know what he was expecting of me. After all, Los Angeles is crawling with agents representing would-be actors. "Why do you want me to represent you?" I asked.

"I want an agent who knows . . ." He paused, lifted his right hand to his cheek, rubbed it up and down as if he were trying to force out the right words. ". . . sports *and* entertainment, and also with a knowledge of endorsements. Too many sports agents think they can push their way into the entertainment field. They make a mistake and I'm the one who's gotta pay for it . . ."

Fred was an agent's dream, but for an agent to sit still and listen is very hard. Agents are hyper types, always moving, always pushing, always talking. However, I sat still and listened to Dryer because he knew what he was talking about; it was his life and he had thought it out.

"When I leave football, I don't have to panic. I've saved my money. I don't have to do anything I don't want to do. I can choose my destiny."

He was lucky money wasn't a problem. He was single, had never married, but he didn't run around like some of the high-living bachelors in the sports scene. He had invested his money in California real estate, and in the past few years, the land values had vastly increased. He could live off his investments. But when his playing days were over, he just didn't want to pack it in and say, "That's the end of my life." He wanted to do something, be part of something. He had trained himself to be a great football player; could he train himself to be a great actor?

"So why do you want *me*?" I repeated.

"I need someone who will guide me to the right jobs. I don't want to rush into anything and blow my chances. I don't want to get a reputation as a football player who wants to play at acting."

"What do you know about acting?"

"A little," he said sheepishly, his face moving in all directions. "Lou Asner suggested I go take lessons."

"Who'd he suggest?"

"Nina Foch."

"Good choice!" Nina Foch is one of Hollywood's best-known acting teachers, and if he wasn't going to make it, she wouldn't keep him on. "Why don't you study with her?"

"I'm going to try."

"Look, Fred," I said, "after Sunday, the football season's over. Take classes. See how you feel about acting. See what Nina says. Do it for a year, find out if acting is what you really want to do, and then we'll go to the networks."

As it turned out, an opportunity to make it on the networks arose before the full year was up. In the beginning of the summer, I started hearing stories. I was having lunch at the Polo Lounge with Milt Suchin, an agent who once headed ICM's (International Creative Management) personal appearance department. He was now on his own, representing such actors and entertainers as Phyllis Diller, Rip Taylor, and Carol Lawrence. Over lunch, Milt told me that his fiancée, Vicki Rosenberg, head of one of the casting departments at NBC, was asking about Vince Ferragamo—and Fred Dryer.

I began thinking. Did we have to wait a year? Fred *had* been taking acting lessons. Perhaps a screen test would show how far he had gotten and if he really had a future worth pursuing. Maybe *now* was the time to strike. I called Vicki Rosenberg, who got us an appointment with Joel Thurm, overall head of casting at NBC. I'd heard of Thurm; he was a straight shooter. This would be a chance to see if they were really interested in Fred.

Before I met Thurm, I was lucky that I went to see George Wallach. George represents Bruce Jenner and had made all Jenner's deals with NBC.

I walked into Wallach's office in one of my negotiating outfits, a conservative three-piece gray suit. When I told George where I was heading, he burst out laughing. "You're crazy dressing like that. Where do you think you're going? The Harvard Business School?"

I was hurt. That suit had cost me over five hundred bucks— and another hundred to take it in after I'd lost a lot of weight. "What's wrong with the way I look?"

"You want to talk to Joel, right? And you want him to talk to you?"

"Yeah." I was defensive and getting a little nervous.

"Joel has a reputation of wearing Bermuda shorts to his office." George's eyes narrowed in on me. "If you dress like that, he'll talk to your suit and treat you like an IBM salesman."

That's all I had to hear. I rushed back to my hotel and changed into jeans and a sports jacket. Then I picked up Fred and we went to see Joel Thurm.

In New York you demonstrate status in a corporation by occupying a corner office high up, with lots of windows so you can look down on the city and the people below you. And the authoritarian person in that office is expected to look the part with a dark suit and white shirt. In Los Angeles, on the other hand, corporate power is evidenced by huge, spacious offices, the latest in designer furniture, and state-of-the-art electronics scattered about. Your personal power is judged by the degree of casualness you can assert, by taking that chic, elegant setting for granted and almost totally disregarding it.

And Joel's office was impressive: enormous and beautifully appointed—a big desk, two sofas with a coffee table for corner conferences. Thurm had come to Hollywood after casting such Broadway hits as *Hello Dolly* and *Grease*. As head of casting at NBC, his word controlled the livelihood of thousands of people. In his mid-thirties and of medium build, he was well-respected and could afford to be very relaxed, and very tanned because he was very good at what he did. It was obvious he had power in Los Angeles. While his office was shimmering with power symbols, he was wearing a pair of shorts and a T-shirt.

I sighed with relief: thank G-d I had changed!

Fred and I had barely gotten into his office when the door started closing, all by itself. It wasn't until three meetings later that I found out Joel had a button on his desk that opened and closed the door—a trick he had picked up from the legendary Harry Cohn, who once headed and dominated Columbia Pictures.

No question about it, we were in Hollywood! And yet, for all the apparent casualness, Joel didn't waste any time. There was no small talk. I was immediately convinced of his sincerity when he admitted he didn't follow football and didn't know who Fred Dryer was. He got right to the point: "Can Fred act?"

Actually, Thurm liked Fred the minute he laid eyes on him, because he had a problem that Fred could solve. Dryer was thirty-three. Most actors who haven't made it by thirty drop out of the business. Conversely, anyone who has made it is into big money. And very few actors in their thirties are just begnning.

But here was Fred starting his career, accepting the fact that he was a beginner. Not that I wasn't going to try to get him a superstar salary, but what Fred was looking for was the experience and the opportunity. And he was smart enough to know you don't always get paid for an opportunity. Sometimes *you* have to pay for it. But once you get it, it's up to you to cash in on it.

For Joel, Fred presented other advantages. He was an unknown actor but with a well-known name; he was someone who already had national recognition. The result of the meeting was that Joel agreed to submit Fred to all the producers NBC was dealing with.

And true to Joel's words, Fred got work. His first acting role was in *Starmaker*, a Movie of the Week, with Rock Hudson. It was about the life of King Vidor, a famous Hollywood director who married a lot of beautiful women and turned them into movie stars. Fred played the brother and legal guardian of a young girl who got involved with Hudson. *Starmaker* was aired the same night as the Cooney-Norton fight at Madison Square Garden. I was torn between watching my client and tuning in the fight. At a station break and during the commercial, I quickly flicked from the movie to Home Box Office (HBO) just in time to catch the bell for the first round. I watched Cooney put Norton away in fifty-six seconds, then got right back to Fred without missing a thing. It was great: the best of two worlds.

Fred then did *The Kid from Nowhere*, starring Loretta Swit, about a mentally retarded child and the Special Olympics. One Tuesday night, after the movie was wrapped, I got a call from Beverly Nix, a business manager at Warner Brothers. Warner's was producing a new *Maverick* series for NBC. James Garner was going to star again as Bret Maverick, and the movie studio was interested in Fred co-starring as Bret's partner. Dryer would tend bar, be around to sympathize and help the ladies who would fall over themselves for Bret. He would also help Bret solve crimes.

Beverly wanted to work out a deal over the phone. But this was a very big step for Fred, and we both felt I had to be there. This was Tuesday; Warner's had booked a screen test for Friday. I caught a plane to the Coast, arriving on Wednesday morning.

The people at Warner's were spending a lot of time with Fred. They wanted him to work on the part, and he did, going over the script again and again. But before the test, they wanted Fred to sign a memo agreement spelling out the terms of the contract if they decided to use him.

I questioned their tactics in wanting to negotiate *before* the test. Then I found out the reason.

The networks had learned their lesson when Farrah Fawcett took her screen test for *Charlie's Angels.* At that time, the rule was that first you test. If the studio is interested, then you negotiate a contract. Farrah was sensational. A decision was made that they had to have her. But she got wind of their committed position, held them up in negotiations, and won because the studio had no leverage. They weren't ever going to make that mistake again.

When I arrived in Los Angeles on Wednesday, I went straight to the office of John Thomas, Fred Dryer's lawyer and a longtime friend. Fred joined us, and the three of us discussed the negotiating tactics we would use and how to handle the meeting. We decided that I, as the agent, would do all the talking, and John would sit silently, digesting and analyzing the information.

Warner's opening bid was a thirteen-week contract for $5,000 an episode. Twenty-two weeks is a full season; Hollywood arithmetic makes thirteen weeks a half season. But one of the good things about Hollywood is that it's a small town, and there's always someone who is willing to talk out of school. I had already heard that even though the series was contracted only for thirteen episodes, Garner had been guaranteed a salary for twenty-two weeks. NBC was hedging their bets; if the show failed, they would only have to pay Garner for the full season and could drop everyone else. If it succeeded, NBC had their star locked up for a full season and everyone else naturally would stay on.

My negotiating point was that Fred needed the security of a full season *guaranteed.* If he got the part, he would have to start shooting right away—which meant he would have to retire from football, which in turn meant giving up a salary of $200,000 plus on a no-cut contract.

"But he's new in the business," the Warner people kept saying. "He's a novice."

"Novice?" My voice went up a little as if I were insulted. "If he's such a novice, why do you want him to co-star?"

Warner's didn't answer.

"Look," I went on, "he's a known name. He was in *Starmaker, The Kid from Nowhere.* His national Bic shaving commercial is airing, and I just got him a guest star appearance on *Laverne and Shirley.*"

We went back and forth, getting nowhere. Little did I realize they were stalling because they had something on me.

It was already late Thursday afternoon, and I had a plane reservation to return to New York later that night. I make it a point to be home with my wife, Monica, and our daughter, Shira, for the Jewish Sabbath. Warner's knew of my religious convictions, so they kept stretching out the time, hoping I would relent in order to catch my plane. It had worked with many people many times before.

"Look," I said finally, "either we make a deal on twenty-two weeks, or we leave."

Now it was John Thomas's turn to speak. "Fred has a contract with the Rams. You don't want him? Fine! He's already a superstar playing football!"

The Warner people didn't like the implied threat and got angry. But we weren't threatening, only telling them the way it was.

"Let's take a break," I said. It was time for a breather before the negotiations froze solid.

John and I conferred out in the hall. We both agreed that Fred was a bit ambivalent about taking this role so soon. It meant going from being All-Pro in one field to being an amateur in another. He had his contract with the Rams; at the same time, he was also taking acting lessons—and getting roles. He could easily go on being an athlete *and* still act. Most important, Freddie could afford to wait. He was getting better at acting, and if he didn't get his big break now, it would come later.

Perhaps the walls at Warner's have ears. When we got back to the table, the studio people were suddenly friendly, and we hammered out an agreement: $12,500 an episode, with escalation clauses for five years. Our agreement, of course, was conditional on Fred's acceptance.

I called Fred at Stenner's and asked him to stay put. John and I rushed over there. Fred asked Stenner to join us, and we went over the pros and cons of the agreement. We all thought it was a good deal.

It was already 9:10 P.M. I called Beverly Nix at home and told her we would accept. John Thomas would go with Fred the next morning and review the memo agreement before Fred signed it.

I caught the "Red Eye" to New York, and Fred took his screen test the next day.

Normally you get an answer to a test in six days. But two weeks passed and we still hadn't heard from Warner's.

Now, suddenly, we were in a dilemma. The football season was just around the corner. Fred had to report to training camp, and he needed to get himself psyched up to go. He couldn't go in thinking about the possibility of walking out should the *Maverick* deal come through. He had to make a clear-cut decision: either to act or play football.

I called Warner's and told them Fred didn't want to play football off against acting. Unless we heard from them in two days, Fred would exercise his option to get out of the agreement and play football that year.

Warner's hemmed and hawed and asked for an extension. After a couple of days of additional calls, we mutually agreed to forget the whole deal.

As I said, Hollywood is a small town, and eventually you hear the reasons for everything. Word got back to me that at first, before the test, James Garner had been all excited about Fred. Garner was an avid football fan and Dryer was a hero in Los Angeles. But after seeing the screen test, Garner got worried. Fred looked taller, stronger, better looking than Garner and, as the star, he naturally wanted to be the center of the action. Here was the co-star's classic problem: You want him to do the job but not compete against the star.

Garner eventually selected Ed Bruce, a country-and-western singer who was short and, in my opinion, not the good-looking Hollywood type.

As things turned out, Garner got injured on the set and the series was delayed until the second half of the season. Had Fred decided to act in the series, he would have given up playing football that year and wound up with nothing.

He returned to training camp expecting to play for two or three more years. Acting would have to wait. But Fred was in for a rude shock. One day at the Rams' training complex, Ray Malavasi, the team coach, walked up to him and said, "Empty your locker." Just like that!

Fred stared at him in disbelief.

"Empty it!" Malavasi ordered and stalked away.

The next morning, Fred came back to camp with his lawyer, John Thomas, who was holding his contract with its no-cut clause in it.

But the Rams didn't talk to Thomas or Dryer, and Fred didn't play football that year. He *did* have a no-cut clause, except that the Rams' general manager, Don Klosterman, forgot to read the contract before he ordered Fred cut. Now, Fred is suing the Rams. As for his acting, it has gotten better and better. He has appeared in *Cheers* and is working on a pilot for a new TV series.

You must know where you want to go with your life. You must set future goals for yourself, as well as the steps along the way that will ensure the future. Everything should be negotiated with those future goals in mind.

Learn to Listen

When you do business, it's vital to know what the other side is *really* saying. With Fred Dryer, I sat and listened; he told me not only what he wanted, but why he wanted me as his agent. I'd say three quarters of successful negotiating depends on knowing *what* the other side wants and *why*.

The problem is that most people are so bent on getting *their* points across they never listen.

Don't Interrupt

When you are negotiating, never interrupt people sitting across from you. For one thing, you want to hear them all the way through so that you can understand their position. For another, you never know where they might be heading. By interrupting them, you not only irritate them (do *you* like being interrupted?), you stop the flow of their thoughts. They may never get back to where they were going.

Instead of interrupting, take notes—of what the person is saying and of questions or statements you want to make. Then when your opponent is finished, you can go back over the areas in question.

Anatomy of a Business Relationship

If you plan to get involved with someone, as I did with Fred Dryer, you have to look at that individual and yourself and consider your mutual plans for today and tomorrow. Something that sounds terrific today may prove embarrassing and even harmful down the road.

Look at the situation when I met Fred. He knew what he wanted for the future: to be an actor. So his plan for *today* was to get into the business slowly, building credits in order to have a foundation. He saw me as someone who could help him make the transition from sports to show business because I was familiar with both fields. I've always felt that if I'm going to be an athlete's agent, it's important that my contribution to that individual must be as strong as his to me. It's no good if you don't have a two-way street.

When you deal with people, figure out where you fit into their entire operation. If you are talking with a very large company, you have much less room to negotiate than if you are dealing with a smaller organization. An individual has more at stake, and your leverage and ability to negotiate are much greater.

Also, who you do business with reflects on you. You must understand this most important aspect of a relationship: Perhaps someone can make you a lot of money today, but down the road, will your association or relationship still be an advantage? If not, then you must weigh the options.

Ask Questions

I always question new clients to find out what they want from me, and what kind of relationship they're expecting in the years to come. No matter what statements you've heard about what people want, don't *ever* assume anything. By asking them and getting their answers, you build an honest relationship from the beginning. To achieve the maximum success through negotiations, you have to know what the other person wants from the relationship, and why. If you go into it selfishly, only for what *you* want, it will turn out to be a no-win situation.

Financial Security

Many people make decisions because of their immediate financial needs. They can't stop to think about the future because they have no cushion to sit on. And so they are forever making decisions to satisfy *today*'s needs.

It is almost impossible to negotiate successfully without some leverage. For most of us, that leverage is financial security. Fred had a football contract; more than that, he had investments to fall back on. The goals he set for himself were attainable because he had financial security while he was working toward what he wanted to do in the future. I tell all my clients to take a percentage of their salary and put it away in a CD, a blue-chip investment, or a money-market fund. If you haven't got that much money, put it in a savings account, or in a Christmas or Hanukkah Club account! You must have *some* financial security; it gives you the edge on getting what you deserve in all other endeavors.

The only way you will have a satisfactory future is to make intelligent decisions today. It's much easier to create a destiny for yourself if you have choices. And financial security gives you the freedom to negotiate your future.

Use of Time

The secret to accomplishing your goals is to set a time limit, and then stick to it.

With all my clients, I plan both a long-range goal of ten years and a short-range goal of five years. The five-year goal is the jumping-off point, the acquisition of the skills and accomplishments that will ensure the fulfillment of the ten-year goal.

Once you have a goal, everything you do must be put in the perspective of reaching it. This holds true whether you are negotiating for a car, a house, a raise, a new job. You must understand the repercussions of *all* your negotiations. How will they affect you today? Tomorrow? Will they advance you to your jumping-off point? Will they lead you into the future?

As long as you have a goal in mind, you can turn your life around at any point. Sometimes you have to swallow hard and do something that seems beneath you. At times, you have to say no when everything in you wants to say yes. Disciplining your ego isn't always easy, but you have to do it if you're looking at a long-term goal.

A Second Job

There are so many benefits resulting from having a second job: money in the bank, tax advantages from an IRA or investment credits. But most important, it gives you leverage in negotiating your business and personal lives. Burgess Owens put it succinctly: "There is no security in football. Even a good football player has only so many years. A second job gives him an option to make the best use of his years."

Burgess was a free safety with the New York Jets before he was traded to the Oakland (now Los Angeles) Raiders. He had been an active member of the race committee of the National Football League Players Association (NFLPA), and he believes he was traded because he had sounded off about "white positions"— quarterbacks, centers, tackles, middle linebackers, and coaches all seemed to be white.

Burgess then got involved in Amway as a salesman. He says Amway helped him set goals, goals that he had to achieve for himself. He became his own boss and felt great about it; his future growth was predicated on his *own* efforts. His rewards were commensurate with whatever efforts he made; he was able to aim for the sky. He had something other than football. So when he got traded, he was able to negotiate a terrific contract with Al Davis with a clear head; his whole life wasn't on the line.

Amway gave him the potential of making as much money as football. But it also made him a better football player, because he had *real* financial security for the rest of his life. His tenth year in the NFL was his best; he played with a greater intensity, not having to worry if his wife and kids would eat or have a place to sleep if he got hurt.

A lot of people—football players are just one example—get so keyed into one profession, they don't see anything else, and then if anything happens, they're in trouble. There is no security in

any one job. By having a second job, you are better able to negotiate what you want out of life.

Identity

People allow themselves to get pegged. With the Rams in the
Super Bowl, Fred Dryer was flooded with opportunities to appear on TV and in the movies. These offers—exploiting him as a
football player—would have been perfectly all right if he hadn't
wanted to be an actor. But with his long-range goal, he had to be
very careful in what he selected, lest he get tagged as a football
player pretending to be an actor. He had to avoid looking like a
guy using his temporary sports notoriety to muscle his way into
acting. If people saw him coming through that way no one would
look at his acting.

Fred was prepared to give himself five years to develop the
acting skills he needed. From the day we started talking seriously, he considered himself a novice in the business. He would
start slow, develop his talents, and build credits as an actor. Because he had money in the bank, he didn't have to take parts that
wouldn't give him legitimate acting credits. He was prepared to
forgo his superstar status in order to build an acting career. And,
as you saw, Fred was as good as his word.

The question of identity and goals applies to most of us: What is
your identity in what you do? I don't mean if you're a secretary, a
bookkeeper, or a small-business man—that's a job title. How are
you identified? Are you honest, aggressive, passive? Do you see
things through? What *attitudes* describe the way you perform?

Ego is not involved here; in fact, you have to try to put ego in
the background. Don't take a position that puts you in a corner: "I
am this, therefore I must get such and such." It's very, very difficult to move from a bunker. If you come on strong, or if you
maintain a position that you will not budge from, you may turn off
the person you are negotiating with. Then what good is your supposed strength?

Before even thinking of assuming a position, you have to ask
yourself what your interests are. Look at whatever you are negotiating and determine what you *want* to get out of the negotiations. What is the other side getting out of it? And the same
questions must be phrased with regard to both your long-term

and short-term goals. They should determine your interests at any given moment; and also determine and dictate the identity you must assume in any negotiation. Typecasting is hard to break out of, and not just in show business. The only way to avoid it is to know what you want today, and what your long-range goal is.

Nothing Is Forever

Many players' associations have accepted the fact that athletes need a transition period from sports to the business world, and they are trying to get assistance for the players from the various professional sports leagues. The same idea applies to all people who are in transition, always moving from today to tomorrow. George Young, general manager of the New York Giants, has acknowledged this problem and has hired career-guidance counselors to work with the players.

Dressing and Grooming

There are many popular books on dressing for success. One additional pointer that I have learned from the world of show business is that when negotiating, I have to dress as close as possible to the other side. If you are dressed inappropriately, it's very possible to send the wrong signals to your opponent and lead the conversation away from the real issues.

What you have to do, of course, is find out who the other side is. To this day, I don't believe Joel Thurm and I would have gotten along if I had been wearing a suit and tie. Possibly he would have felt uncomfortable, and that what I was asking for was excessive. You want the person you are negotiating with to deal with you and the points of mutual discussion, not with the clothes you are wearing.

Equally important, if not more so, is neatness in your personal appearance. If you are neat, this projects thought, care, and consideration about the way you look. The signal you send out is that you will bring that same precision to whatever business is being negotiated—a very important signal to your opponent.

Time Pressure

With Dryer, Warner Brothers intended to use the pressure of time to get me to agree to what they wanted. I had to deal with the next five years of my client's life. I couldn't turn them down, but I couldn't give in either. Most important, I couldn't panic from the pressure they were putting on me when they made their quick call on Tuesday to the East Coast.

I have often felt that my being on the East Coast makes it easier for me to represent West Coast stars. The distance gives me time to think out the pros and cons. I'm not forced into an immediate meeting where I could make the wrong decision. They're not sitting on top of me, nor am I being bombarded with items in the local newspapers to get me to believe things that may not be happening.

When big business confronts you with a deadline, it's very hard to negotiate. First, big business interests *are* impressive, important, and powerful. You do want to do business with those interests. Second, you tend to feel they're so big you'll never get what you want from them anyway.

Accept neither of these two ideas. Express yourself, test your opponent.

Whatever you are negotiating, refuse to accept a deadline. *Create* an excuse to extend your allotted time. This not only will give you time to think, it will show you how serious the other side is about you. Remember, if you're important enough for them to want you, they will wait.

As for revealing your deadline, that's a terrible mistake. You saw what happened to me.

Immediate Sacrifices for Long-Range Goals

As I've said before, you must weigh *everything* you do with regard to your long-range goals. If you have no long-range goals and an opportunity is presented to you, you will take it. You will spend your time and money because you have nothing better to do. But *if you do have something better* to achieve down the line, the decision is not very difficult. You will know exactly when and how and where to spend your time and money.

Handling Put-Downs

Always expect the other side to belittle whatever skills, goals, and success you are trying to sell or negotiate for. You'll hear remarks like "You're a novice, a beginner," and so forth. You have

to be prepared for these remarks. There is no sense in trying to
prove someone is or is not at the novice level. What you do is turn
the negative words around, make them all positive, and use them
for yourself, as I did by asking, "If Fred is such a novice, why do
you want him?"

Now it's the other side's turn to justify why they want someone
or something. And their reasons will reveal to you the degree of
their commitment.

Breaks

If you feel the negotiations are going nowhere, it's very helpful
to take a break. But make sure it's just a *short* break. You don't
want to forget the subject and have to come back and rehash everything. Get up, move around, take a walk, go have a cup of
coffee, go to the bathroom. Stretch your legs physically, and your
brain mentally. Give yourself time to work out in your own mind
the repercussions of what's being offered.

Getting Locked into the Future

In the summer months, one of the most common headlines to
come out of Hollywood concerns stars of top TV series threatening to hold out. Well-known items in the past involved Gary
Coleman of *Diff'rent Strokes*, Suzanne Somers of *Three's Company*, and Erik Estrada of *CHiPs*. The stars' frustrations begin
when the studio locks them up before their show has become a
success. It is quite normal for a producer to offer the studio the
series based on a five-year budget. The producer commits himself
to a certain scale for his actors and actresses. At that time, there is
no way of knowing whether the show will be a success. So, the
actors and actresses accept the figure.

If the show goes over big, the producer winds up making a
bundle. Naturally the stars want to get a bigger fee for themselves
than they have been getting in the past. The producer, having a
contract that calls for a smaller salary scale in comparison to the
success he's had with the show now turns around and says, "We
got a contract."

As Herschel Bernardi put it, "There is a ladder: At the bottom
is the actor or the actress, then the agent, the business manager,
the lawyer, the publicity people, the producer, the studio head,

the network programmer, and the president of the network. Talent is at the bottom of the ladder and, consequently, the least powerful." What you have to do—not only if you are an actor or an actress, but in anything in life—is negotiate on the assumption that whatever you are getting into *is* going to be a success. Therefore, you want protection for the future. It is almost impossible to estimate future success. However, one way around the problem is the escalation clause: If certain things happen (a week on the best-sellers list, earnings over two million dollars), then there will be a fixed increase in compensation.

Escalation is a very positive tool to use in negotiation. On the one hand, it gives you protection if you come up with a winner. On the other hand, you're telling whomever you are negotiating with that the project *is* going to be a success. And that as the success becomes greater, so does your stake, and therefore you're financially motivated to give it everything you've got.

Escalation clauses are the only solution to your "problem" of future success. But make sure that all such promises wind up in writing.

CHAPTER

3

SHOW BIZ

One day, after I first opened my own office, I got a call from the Fort Lauderdale Hebrew Day School. They were putting on a Sunday benefit concert at the Fort Lauderdale Playhouse and needed an entertainer, "someone who can draw."

One of the great advantages I saw when I started in the business of being an agent was that I could select the celebrities *I* wanted to meet. For a long time I had wanted to meet Herschel Bernardi. I found out that Bernardi's price at the time was $7,500 a show (now it's $12,000). But I had been warned off. A lot of people told me he had a very powerful attorney in Los Angeles who did all his bookings. So when the school in Fort Lauderdale called, I immediately asked them if they would be interested in Bernardi.

"Of course!" was the answer. "How much?"

"Seventy-five hundred."

"Too much."

"But you want a draw. Bernardi's a draw."

"Too much. All our budget calls for is fifty-five."

That seemed to be the end of my chance to meet Bernardi.

Two days later I got a call from Sid Levenson of The Ark. The Ark is a charitable organization that helps the Jewish poor in the Chicago area. Levenson wanted a well-known celebrity for a concert. He gave me the date and told me the concert was going to be at the Mill Run Theater.

After I hung up, I looked at the date and realized it was the same day as the benefit in Fort Lauderdale. I went back over my notes; the Florida concert would be in the afternoon, the Chicago concert in the evening.

My head began to run at full steam. I asked my secretary to get the plane schedules from Fort Lauderdale to Chicago for that day, and sure enough, there was an early evening flight that could get Bernardi into Chicago in time for the show.

Could I put Bernardi in two spots halfway across the country on the same day? I learned that kind of scheduling in the Catskills. You book an entertainer for two shows for one day, and you get a better price; you save the hotel some money and the entertainer makes a little more. This was a little different—two different spots fifteen hundred miles apart—but it was the same principle.

Could I do it? I was sure as hell going to try. So I got up my courage and called Bernardi's people in Los Angeles.

"Hi, this is David Fishof. I spoke to you two days ago about booking Herschel Bernardi."

"Yes," said Darlene Lancer, one of the attorneys handling Bernardi.

"You said the price is seventy-five hundred."

"That's right."

"Would he be interested in ten thousand for the *day?*"

"Ten thousand dollars?" I figured Bernardi would make more than he normally gets, and the two organizations would have a top draw for only $5,000 apiece.

"Ten thousand dollars," I reiterated quickly.

"For the day?" She had picked up on my careful wording. "What do you mean for the day?"

"It's two spots. The one in Fort Lauderdale I spoke to you about, and there's one in Chicago that evening. I checked it out. He'll have no trouble making the flight to Chicago."

"I'll get back to you," she told me.

So I waited excitedly. Here it was my first week in business, and I had a chance of booking $10,000 for one day. My commission was going to be $1,000, and I'd done it all over the phone without even meeting the people—some jump from running around the Catskills!

In half an hour, I got a call back. "David? This is Darlene Lancer."

"Hi."

"It's a deal. Ten thousand, pay or play."

"You got it," I said quickly, without even considering what she was saying to me. "Pay or play" means the performer gets the agreed-on salary for that date no matter what—even if the concerts are canceled.

In two days I got the contracts from Bernardi's attorney, Marvin Sears, and sure enough, it was "pay or play." Before I signed the contract, I called up both organizations to be sure they were still interested. I got a yes from both. I had contracts typed out for each of the organizations and mailed them out. Then I signed the contract for Bernardi and sent it to his attorney. I figured all I had to do was wait for the contracts from Fort Lauderdale and Chicago to come back, and I'd be a thousand dollars richer.

Of course, I had made a terrible mistake. I had committed myself to Bernardi for $10,000 *before* the two organizations had committed themselves contractually. I put myself out on a limb, hoping the two would come through. Well, I was young, anxious, and excited about doing this kind of business.

The contract from The Ark came back immediately, but not the one from Fort Lauderdale. I telephoned.

"Don't worry," the guy told me. "They're going to sign the contract today and put it in the mail."

Days went by and still no contract. I kept calling Fort Lauderdale, and all I got was the same response: "It's in the mail." But now I was getting the answer not from the man but from his secretary. Suddenly I was worried. "It's in the mail" means it's nowhere.

I sent a telegram to Fort Lauderdale. Finally I got a call from an officer of the organization who informed me they couldn't organize the ticket committee. Because they couldn't sell enough tickets, they had canceled the show.

I called Darlene in California. "Fort Lauderdale just canceled on me. So I only have one show. Would Bernardi do it for five thousand?"

"No," she said. "He's getting ten thousand for the day. That's what we've signed on. We have a contract."

"But Fort Lauderdale canceled."

"Look." Darlene was not the least bit sympathetic to my problem. "I don't care if you have one show, two shows, or *no* shows. We agreed on ten thousand dollars."

I hung up the phone and looked around my small office. Was it all over so fast? Here I was with a client in Chicago who was advertising Herschel Bernardi's concert; I'd committed Bernardi. I was facing a Beverly Hills law firm that had a reputation in show business as a tough negotiator. I could hear Darlene's words ringing in my ears: "We have a deal . . . ten thousand dollars." I was twenty years old and still going to college in the mornings. I only had $2,500 in my savings account. What was I going to do? I knew the entire time Darlene had been consulting with Marvin Sears.

My eyes roamed around my office as I looked for a way out of the situation, hoping some answer would jump out of the walls and save me. It looked hopeless. I couldn't ask Chicago for more money; a deal is a deal. To keep my reputation alive, I could pay the difference out of my pocket—although I didn't have it all. Or I could cancel Bernardi and face a lawsuit, and then my reputation in California would be zero. The last option was no way to get started in big-time show biz. And this was the business I wanted to be in.

I realized I wasn't going to get answers by staring at the walls in my office. I started making phone calls to people in the business. I also kept hearing how excited Bernardi was about doing the show. He was telling all his friends about going to Florida and Chicago. Why?

"You see," a friend of Bernardi's said to me, "usually he does *Fiddler on the Roof* and he gets a standing ovation. But who are they really applauding—Herschel or *Fiddler?* What he really wants is his own cabaret show. He wants people to applaud him, not *Fiddler;* him, the performer. That's why he's so excited."

Later I found out he was excited because he hadn't worked—as a live entertainer—in a long time. He was making a great deal of money doing voice-overs for TV commercials—for Zenith, as Charlie the Tuna, as the Jolly Green Giant—but no live shows. (Since then, he has been working constantly.)

I couldn't believe what I was hearing. I was sitting here worrying, hoping he'd do me a favor, but it seems I was doing *him* a favor. So I definitely couldn't cancel him. The opportunity was too important for me, too. Now I knew that Bernardi wanted to go on, could I use that to end-run Sears?

I called California and spoke to Darlene. "We have the show in Chicago. I'll give Bernardi six thousand for it. That's it. If you don't want the six, I'm canceling."

We went through the same routine: she saying I signed for ten and me saying one of the shows had canceled. Finally I said, "Look! Forget it—even the one show. It's not worth the hassle. I'm canceling out. You can sue me."

I held my breath. If she hung up, I might as well pack it in. I was going to be sued—and get killed.

"Let me get back to you," she said.

I couldn't help but smile to myself as I hung up. I knew I had done it. I imagined the whole time that she was telling Bernardi the problem. Sure enough, a few hours later Darlene called back and we struck a deal—settled!

Three days before the performance, I got a call. "David?"

I didn't recognize the voice. "Yes?"

Suddenly there was laughter at the other end of the phone. "I gotta hand it to you. You really did a number on my attorney."

Now I recognized the voice. Herschel Bernardi.

"I've asked around about you," he went on. "I'm told you're a young fellow. Bright. I've heard a lot of nice things about you. I want to meet you."

"Anytime." My heart was beating fast; he was the man *I* wanted to meet. Now *he* wanted to meet me.

"Come visit me," Bernardi said. "Fly to Chicago."

Before the show in Chicago, we went to a Chinese restaurant across the street from the Mill Run Theater. I didn't eat anything because I'm kosher. But Bernardi ate, talking between mouthfuls.

"I want you to handle me. Be my agent."

I'm glad I wasn't eating; I would have choked. "How come?"

Bernardi smiled. "Listen, anyone who can go up against my attorney and get me here today is someone I want to represent me."

"Great!" I was so excited, ecstatic, that that was all I could say.

"I need an agent, a young fellow like you who will push for me."

I was honored. "How do we get it going?"

"I want you to come to Los Angeles. Meet my lawyer, Marvin Sears."

I gulped. Seeing the look on my face, Bernardi reached out across the table and patted my arm. "He's a nice man, David. You'll like him!"

Nice man? He was the meanest man I had ever spoken to over the telephone. But then again, I was used to dealing with a different type of person. This was my first exposure to a class operator. He wasn't mean, he was protecting his client.

Bernardi did the show. More important, I had him as a client. (And The Ark invited him back the next two years at double the price.)

The following week I flew to Los Angeles and checked into the Century Plaza Hotel. Quickly I changed my clothes and headed for my 1:30 appointment with Marvin Sears.

The firm of Pacht, Ross, Warne, Bernhard, and Sears occupies two full floors in Century City. I had to go through a long corridor to Sears's office, and I felt I was running a gauntlet.

The first thing I saw in Marvin's office was his desk—a massive, solid piece of wood—with no drawers, only a telephone console built into it. And all around the room were show business memorabilia of his clients, and lots of Bernardi items.

Sears is a tall, slim, grayish-brown-haired man, about fifty years old. With his half-rim glasses and conservative suit and tie, he is a very authoritative figure.

Bernardi made the introductions. "Nice to meet you," Marvin Sears said and I returned the greeting, but neither of us was really sincere, just polite. Bernardi motioned me to a chair across the desk from Marvin, and then sat off to the side. During the meeting he never said another word; he just sat there, listened, and smiled.

Something told me Marvin wasn't as distant as he seemed. There was no anger in him, no hostility. You must remember, I was a little concerned after all I had heard about him. But then I thought, he wouldn't have allowed this if he really thought it was bad for him and Bernardi. After all, he still had Herschel as a client; they were still friends. Why did he need to be his agent, too?

We chatted about the kinds of work Herschel would like to do, and we came up with ground rules for my representing him.

"One thing you have to understand," Marvin said. "We either get our price for our shows, or we don't perform."

"I understand that," I said in all sincerity.

"I want to be sure you do, *David*." His voice was cool. "As for a contract . . ."

"No," I interrupted him, "I don't need a contract. I trust you guys."

Marvin peered over his glasses at me. "We work with contracts, David. We'll write one up for you, and we want you to sign it because you're going to be Herschel's representative. From now on, any phone calls I get, I'll refer to you. But if someone wants us"—he constantly used the word *us*, letting me know it was him and Bernardi—"they must pay our rate or we won't work."

That was my first lesson in big-time show business. I was used to the small-time finagling I had learned from "dealing with" the smaller Catskills hotels. This was different.

"Fine," I said. "I understand."

"Good. Now our price is seventy-five hundred a show . . ."

He then proceeded to give me a rundown on the "extras." Herschel does most of his shows with a piano player. So there must be a suite for Bernardi and a single room for the piano player. "There has to be a limo picking him up at the airport and taking him back and, of course, two first-class plane tickets."

Later I asked Herschel why the big deal about the suite and the limo.

"David," he said, "you know what happens to the money for the performance? It goes to Marvin. He invests it for me. Every once in a while I find out I own another store in a shopping mall. But it's not money that makes you a star. It's the way they treat you."

"And so the suite and the limo."

"Right. They treat you like a star, and I give them star performances." Several years later, the comedian Fred Travalena would tell me the same thing about being a star. There's a difference if they send a car to pick you up. It's a caste system: A limo has status and you get treated differently; you get more respect. "David," said Herschel, his eyes full of warmth, "I'm a simple guy. Look at me." Suddenly he looked like Tevye. "David, do I need that kind of stuff?"

Marvin sent me a contract and we were in business. I immediately called my friend Jerry Weiss at Grossinger's. "Jerry? How would you like Bernardi for Passover? I represent him now."

"I'd love him! How much?"

"Seventy-five hundred." And then I added quickly, "Plus two first-class airfares from Los Angeles, a suite and a single, and a limo back and forth to New York."

"Come on, David," Jerry said. "We're old friends. You know I can't pay that kind of money."

"How much can you pay?" I asked, so excited about booking Bernardi that I forgot what Marvin Sears had told me. I still had my "Catskills mentality." In the Catskills, you see, there's always petty bargaining, like: "Okay, you can't give me a first-class ticket, give me coach. You can't give me that suite, give me a single."

"How much can I pay?" Jerry repeats my question. "Three thousand."

"No way!"

"Okay. Five thousand, David. That's tops!"

I was so busy figuring out my 10 percent commission, I hadn't remembered Marvin's rule. You must remember, I had been selling acts into the Catskills for $150, $200, $350 a night. I still didn't know what big-time show business was all about. Suddenly I was being *offered* $5,000 and, of course, I jumped at it. "I'll get back to you," I told Jerry and immediately got on the phone to Bernardi. "I have an offer from Grossinger's for Passover."

"Terrific," Bernardi said. "I knew you could do it. You got me everything we talked about?"

I was hesitant, but then I finally blurted out, "They only want to pay five thousand."

Bernardi was angry. "David, we made a deal. Have you forgotten what we talked about?"

As soon as I got off the phone with Bernardi, I called Grossinger's back and told Jerry either to pay the price or forget about it. He went up to $6,500. Then I called Marvin, thinking I could convince him to let me book Herschel for $6,500. "Come on. Let's take it. We can't get any more."

Marvin heard me out then said, "David, if you are going to be Herschel's agent, you have to do it right." He was patient with me, not angry, not even scolding . . . teaching. "I'm telling you. Either we get the price, or we don't do it. If Grossinger's wants Herschel, tell them his price. They have to pay that. If they don't want him, *don't worry.* We don't need the job. Herschel's worked for many years, and he's saved his money. He likes to work, but if they don't pay his price, he's not going to do it."

I sat there listening. There was no sense arguing. I knew I was getting good advice, and that I had to change my style. Marvin was telling me simply that I was there to work for *Herschel,* not for myself. I could make money on him, but only at *his* price.

"Herschel is independent," Marvin went on. "He can choose his work." Marvin paused. "But you know what?"

"What?" I asked.

"He always comes out the winner. If they want Bernardi's type, there's only one Herschel Bernardi."

I sat in my office, torn in two. I wanted—NEEDED—to book Bernardi into Grossinger's to prove I was on my way up. I was prepared to take less to get that chance, but Marvin wouldn't let me sell Bernardi for less than his price. I had yet to learn a truism of this business: To be a good agent, it was my role not just to get a job for my client, but to get the best possible deal.

I called Jerry again. "Jerry, what's happening?"

"I have a meeting with Paul Grossinger in an hour. I'll call you back."

Two hours later, Jerry called. "Okay, David. We'll take him at his price."

Now I called Marvin back, my chest swelling with pride. "Marvin, I got it!"

"Fine." Marvin wasn't as excited as I was. "See what I told you? They want him, they pay for him. If they *hadn't* really wanted him, David, they never would have even offered you five thousand dollars."

Monica and I went to Grossinger's to see Herschel. The show was great, but I had forgotten to make sure Herschel had a suite, and he was disappointed in me. "I don't work for a hundred and a quarter," he said, making fun of my Catskills mentality. "A suite is important."

He was right. It was part of my job to be sure he got what we agreed to.

One thing I owe Herschel Bernardi: He took me out of schlock. He kept saying, "David, it's all schlock. I'm going to teach you class." And over the years, he molded me. It took me a while to change, but he did teach me. He's the one client I even let yell at me, because I knew I had plenty to learn.

Marvin Sears and I developed a very close relationship, and I trusted him to represent me as my attorney in many deals, especially concerning the highly complicated clauses in Vince Ferragamo's contract.

Herschel Bernardi and Marvin Sears became mentors to me in this business. They showed me how to climb to a higher level. I found it easier to sell Bernardi at $10,000 a night than to sell a comedian for $125.

Ben Vereen has a clause in his contract that specifies he must have a dozen roses and a basket of fruit in his dressing room. Some performers even specify the kind of mineral water they want. Why? Most of it is to make a performer feel good, wanted, special. If a performer feels he or she is getting second-rate treatment, he or she will go onstage and give a second-rate performance. Bob Hope once told me that his show always reflects how he's treated when he comes in to work. Bob is lucky; he's always treated royally. "But I can tell the difference if they really want me, or if I'm there just to do a job."

Demands—the extras specified by stars—are interesting. The late Harry Chapin was represented by my friend Dennis Arfa, who is now head of the music department at the William Morris Agency. There were clauses in Chapin's contract that detailed the kind of menu—and it had to be a fourteen-course menu—he had to be given, depending on the day he was booked. For instance, if he was booked on a Tuesday, he and his band would have to be served roast turkey with cranberry sauce and mushrooms; Wednesday, it would be steak; Thursday, chicken; Friday, sweetbreads. And the clauses were binding. If the demands weren't there, Chapin had the right to cancel an appearance.

Once I had Ron Eliran, an Israeli performer and close friend of mine, open a show for Bill Cosby in Hartford, Connecticut. Cosby told me that twenty years before, he had opened a show for Ron down in the Village. Now the tables were turned.

Most performers are particular about how much time the opening act takes. They don't want anyone going over twenty minutes—and if the act is too good, it will take away from their performance. But if the act is *bad*, it puts the audience in a lousy mood.

Comic Van Harris told me a story that he was once booked to open at the Concord Hotel for Steve Lawrence and Eydie Gormé. He was advised to do twenty minutes. He stayed onstage for over thirty-five minutes because the audience was roaring and applauding. He walked offstage thinking he was a winner, until Eydie stormed over to him screaming and yelling. It cost him a nationwide tour with the two singers.

Morty Gunty, a successful opening-act comedian, told me his success is due to holding to the time he is given. If told to do nineteen minutes, he will look at a clock—all the clubs in Vegas have a clock on the floor of the stage—and when he sees he has already done eighteen minutes, he will start making his exit even if it's in the middle of a punch line. He does this to keep his commitment. It not only makes the performers happy, it makes the clubs happy. In Vegas, remember, the hotels don't want long shows. They want people to go back into the casinos and gamble.

But Cosby is different about opening acts. "Let them do whatever they want." He's so sure of himself that five minutes before he goes on, he walks into the theater still reading his *New York Times*. "All I need is a mike and a chair." He goes out and does an hour and a half and the audience is roaring.

A favorite of mine is Henny Youngman, the only guy in show business who will be booked into a show as a headliner and then try to be the opening act so he can catch a plane home that night.

We once did a convention in New Jersey, and Henny spoke about me for five minutes, building me up. Then, all of a sudden, he introduced me in front of two thousand people and said, "You see that look on his face? You know why he's so angry?" He paused. "I'm taking ninety percent of his money."

Bob Hope is often introduced as a great American, which is exactly what he is. Home Box Office asked me to get him for a convention. I telephoned him and we agreed on a price for the show. The morning of the show, Bob's conductor flew into Atlanta and I picked him up at the airport.

"Listen," he said to me, "when you talk to Bob, make sure you talk loud because he's getting a little deaf and he doesn't wear a hearing aid. You gotta remember, he's seventy-nine years old."

I made arrangements to pick him up. Just by saying, "I'm picking up Bob Hope," I was able to get the car right out on the runway. He came in on the same plane with Doc Severinsen and Ricky Nelson.

We were sitting in the car, laughing and talking—with me speaking very, very loud—about the L.A. Rams.

"I used to own the Rams," Bob told me. "Why did Ferragamo leave?" Before I could answer, he told me that Elizabeth Taylor once wouldn't let the Rams' owner Georgia Frontiere on one of her specials.

We got to the convention, and he was immediately surrounded by people backstage. He couldn't hear a thing being said to him, but he walked around smiling at everyone. It was marvelous. Sure, it's marvelous—for $50,000 a night.

"Top of the show" is a Hollywood term for the price paid for a leading actor to be a guest on a TV series. One day I got a call for Vince Ferragamo from the casting director of *Laverne and Shirley*.

He offered me $1,000 for one appearance on a half-hour show. I told him I couldn't even take an offer that low to Vince. He would turn it down flat. Over the course of the week we had several conversations, and each time the ante was upped $250 until we finally agreed on $2,500, which came only after I received a call from the producer of the show, and from Penny Marshall herself, asking Vince to appear.

But now Vince did not want to do it. He felt that it would be too much work to do on his day off. This was going to be filmed during the football season. So I asked them if they would take Fred Dryer instead. They agreed and said, "top of the show is a thousand dollars," and they had no more budget.

You can imagine how I felt. I had just been offered $2,500 for the same part. Why not budget the same amount for another player?

Fred Dryer wound up doing the show at the top-of-the-show price: $2,500.

One of the major rules of negotiation is don't accept just because something is offered to you. Test what you're being offered.

CHAPTER

4

YOU CAN GO HOME AGAIN

The clock just kept on ticking. Only minutes remained to the end of the game. Most of the 64,792 football fans who had packed the Texas stadium were Dallas Cowboy fanatics. Time was on their side, and they were winning. They were on their feet, drinking longnecks, hooting and hollering, celebrating their fifth National Football Conference championship. They were certain they were on their way to the Super Bowl.

You couldn't blame them for celebrating. The Cowboys were ahead 19–14. The Los Angeles Rams had the ball on their own thirty. It was a long way downfield, and the Dallas defense was one of the best in the business. They had been here before; they knew how to keep the lid on.

The Rams fans were sitting in their seats, quiet. To them, it looked hopeless. A stillness surrounded the Rams' side of the field, a stillness full of hope, a hush that precedes a storm, or a miracle. And all eyes were watching one man, Vince Ferragamo. It was a storybook situation. Six feet three inches and 210 pounds, Vince has a sultry Italian look. Hollywood would have cast him for the role he was playing, if he weren't in the process of creating it for himself.

When the 1979 season opened, Vince was on the bench, the backup quarterback. Vince thought he should be number one or

at least given a chance to prove himself. The Rams weren't paying much attention to him, however. Word had gone out that
their number one quarterback was going to be Pat Haden, the
squeaky-clean, blond, blue-eyed golden boy from the University
of Southern California (USC).

And so it was. With Haden at the helm, the Rams rushed into
last place in the first half of the season, losing five out of six
games. The fans were screaming for Haden's scalp, but the Rams
wouldn't budge. He was the chosen one.

Lady Luck didn't agree. Haden got injured, and Vince took
over with a vengeance. In the Rams' next seven games, he led
them to six victories. Los Angeles came alive with football fever.
Was it possible? Could they go all the way?

Vince got the team into the play-offs. It was an accomplishment
any man would have been proud of, but for Vince Ferragamo it
was not enough. Determination burned in his eyes, setting everything around him on fire. He had sounded off because he knew he
was good and he was going to show them *all*—the Cowboys, the
fans, and especially the Rams' management.

Now time was running out. Vince started: "Set, forty-nine . . ."
The Rams had the ball on the thirty-yard line. First down with
ten yards to go for another first. But another first wasn't going to
help. They needed a touchdown, a big one; it was now or never.
Vince knew it. Dallas knew it. The wild roaring of the Texas
crowd drowned out half the call.

Vince took the snap from center. Dallas blitzed. Vince stepped
into the pocket. He had a second, maybe two, to get rid of the
ball. He spotted Billy Waddy twenty yards downfield. There was
just enough daylight between Waddy's yellow and blue jersey
and the silver and blue of the Dallas defenders. Vince's eyes
locked onto Waddy as his arm rifled the ball.

Waddy caught it and outran the frantic Dallas safeties the remaining fifty yards to the goal line. *The Rams were on their way
to the Super Bowl.*

In the end they lost to the mighty Pittsburgh Steelers. But they
had been there, and the man who had made it happen—Vince
Ferragamo—was suddenly a very hot item.

Two weeks after the game, I got a call from a fellow saying, "Hi.

My name is Vince Ferragamo. I'm with the Los Angeles Rams. Freddie Dryer suggested I get in touch with you. Everyone's after me to endorse their products. I need some help." He paused, then went on, "I was just in the Super Bowl."

I loved the way he said it. No strutting, just matter-of-fact, sincere. We talked a little, and I asked him to send me all the offers he had gotten.

A day later, a huge envelope from Vince arrived via Federal Express. It contained *hundreds* of offers: for T-shirts, football jerseys with his name on them; there were sneaker deals, clothing deals; an offer of $10,000 to host a stag party; offers for TV and movie appearances, a Walt Disney picture. There was a letter from Salvatore Ferragamo of Ferragamo Shoes asking if they were relatives. There was even an offer to do a pantyhose ad, and one for a baby-oil product with a very seductive connotation.

Most of the merchandise offers were merely promises, contracts saying that Vince would get 6 percent of the gross profit on T-shirts, jerseys, footballs, whatever carried his name. Then in fine print the contracts defined "gross" as whatever money was left after expenses. In other words, he would get very little if he didn't get money up front. But there were also some legitimate offers. I flew out to California to meet Vince. He, his wife, Jodi, and I agreed that I would handle his endorsements and personal appearances.

Vince had come off a great season and was going into his option year. Most general managers like to renegotiate during the option year, and Vince's contract certainly needed renegotiating! He was the lowest-paid quarterback in the NFL. By way of comparison, Archie Manning of the New Orleans Saints, a quarterback who hadn't won a game the year before, was earning $367,000 a year. Vince, who had taken the Rams to the Super Bowl, was earning only $52,000 a year.

Vince thought he was in a strong position. He genuinely expected the Rams would come through with a new contract that was fair and equitable. He asked my advice, but since he already had a lawyer, Paul Caruso, to negotiate for him, I didn't want to get involved and I shied away. You can't have two people negotiating for you. I told him he had to stick with whomever he felt was doing the best job for him, follow that person's advice, and see what he got.

I concentrated on his endorsements. Over the spring and summer, we got some terrific commercials: Sasson Jeans, Pioneer Chicken, Kootsie Cup—a cup in a warmer that had his picture on it. We also got a pair of child's sunglasses called "The Vinnie," an invitation to the White House, and an offer to come to the Superstars.

The endorsements and the appearances were fun, and the money was good. But first and foremost, Vince was a football player. His performance on the field in '79 moved him into the superstar category. In 1980 he went into training camp expecting to get his rewards—the salary he deserved, the position he had earned.

He got neither. The Rams' management just wouldn't give up on Pat Haden. There was no logical explanation. They totally disregarded Haden's losing record and developed acute amnesia about Vince's performance the year before.

There was also the problem of who was really running the Rams. Don Klosterman was the general manager, but the ownership had just changed hands. Carroll Rosenbloom had died, and a will made out two weeks before his death gave 70 percent ownership of the team to his wife, Georgia, and the balance distributed among the five children.

Although I heard rumors about what was happening, I was not yet in the negotiations at this point. No one was talking seriously to Vince or to his attorney, Caruso. The Rams were going to go with Haden, and there was no reason to make a deal with Ferragamo. But no matter what the Rams' management did, it was never in the cards for Haden to make it. He broke his finger in the first game of the season, and once again the Rams called on Vince to come off the bench. Naturally enough, Vince now believed the Rams would sit down and talk about his contract. He was asking for a fair amount and, wanting to play in Los Angeles, sought a contract for several years. Caruso was talking to the Rams and told Vince not to worry. He would take care of it as a favor for a *paisano*, and it wouldn't cost Vinnie a cent.

Halfway through the season, Caruso, Klosterman, and Georgia

were sitting around a table at Scandia, a restaurant on Sunset Boulevard. They struck a deal and shook hands on it. Then Caruso called Vince to tell him what he had agreed to. Vince couldn't believe his ears: $150,000 for the option year he was playing. Then a new three-year contract at $175,000 for the first year, $200,000 for the second year, and $225,000 for the third year.

Caruso was a bit of a publicity hound. When he heard that Haden had been injured and Vince would be playing, Caruso called Vince and told him to walk out of camp and come to his office. Vince protested that he was getting his chance. Why walk out now? But Caruso insisted it would strengthen his hand at the negotiations.

Vince followed Caruso's advice and walked out of camp. When he got to the lawyer's office in Beverly Hills, the place was packed with reporters and photographers. Caruso strode over to Vince and put his arms around him. The flashbulbs went off; that was the picture that made the *Los Angeles Times* the next day. It seemed that was all Caruso was after. Because the next day he told Vince to go back to camp as if nothing had happened.

Meanwhile, the negotiations got nowhere. Vince was getting disgusted and afraid that the prolonged hassling would affect his game. He called me. By this time, we had a relationship based on facts, not promises. He had done all the endorsements and personal appearances I had set up for him. He had confidence in me. After all, he had seen the dollars.

"David," he said, "I want you to handle my negotiations with the Rams."

"What about Caruso?" I asked.

"I'm firing him."

A couple of calls to Klosterman, and I began unraveling the web Caruso had weaved. The story eventually came out when an investigative reporter of *Inside Sports* dug out the truth: Caruso was an old friend of Klosterman's. When Caruso sat down to talk to Klosterman and later with Georgia, he asked the Rams for $50,000 for himself for negotiating Vince's contract. The Rams countered with $25,000. The method of payment, in my opinion, represented a conflict of interest for Caruso.

I suggested to Vince that right now there was too much confusion and bad blood. The best thing was for him to play out the season while I developed a rapport with the Rams.

He agreed, and I started talking with the club, but with very little leverage. After all, Vince was still in his option year; he would be a free agent after the season. But in football the free-agent system doesn't work. If a player moves to another team as a free agent and is paid over $200,000 a year, the new team must give the former team their *first-round draft picks for two successive years*—a ransom worthy of a king. First-round draft picks are the transfusions that create dynasties in ball clubs. And for *two* years? Forget it! Very few clubs would do it. To prove it, it was rumored that Jack Kent Cooke, owner of the Washington Redskins, offered the New England Patriots $2.5 million for a first-round pick in 1982.

If that isn't bad enough, there's another provision that tightens the control over a free agent. The player's former club has the right to match whatever bid the player accepts with another club. And if they do, the player has to go back and play for his former club.

Now here was Vince, who was making $52,000 a year. I told him it would be an easy setup for a club to offer him $100,000, even $150,000, and then have the Rams match it. He would then have to go play for the Rams at that salary. And because the amount was under $200,000, any club who bid for him had nothing to lose because the Rams would pick him up. Nice, huh? A situation ideally made for a little collusion.

We were in a corner. There was no doubt about it. If Vince was to play football in the NFL, he could play only in Los Angeles. What I needed was a real alternative to the NFL.

There was some talk about a new league, and I even got a call from a guy who wanted Vince, but it was all talk. The only alternative was Canada. A lot of guys, especially players who had been cut from the roster, had gone from the NFL to Canada. But a superstar had never gone up there at the height of his fame.

It was a *sensational* handle worth exploring—both as a negotiating tactic against the Rams and as a positive move on Vince's behalf. He was playing his heart out, and, depressingly, there was not the slightest sign of appreciation from the Rams.

I sent telegrams to all the Canadian Football League clubs telling them I represented Vince Ferragamo, who was interested in playing football in Canada. I waited, but nothing happened.

I didn't understand why I got no responses. So I made a few calls, and found out that each team in Canada is allowed the rights to twenty NFL pros and college players. It's called a negotiation list. They just divvy up the players, even if they've never been approached. The Hamilton Tiger-Cats (Hamilton is a steel town outside Toronto) had the rights to Vince.

At first, Ralph Sazio, the Cats' general manager, didn't believe I was serious when I called. Finally I convinced him I was, and I secretly flew to Canada for a meeting in a motel near the Toronto airport. I had to go secretly because I didn't want Klosterman to know I was in Canada, and there is always a reporter around who finds out who is traveling where. Many times, reporters also supply the why—conjecture—and that was something we had to avoid at this stage of the negotiations. Sazio was there, along with the accountant for the Tiger-Cats' owner, Harold Ballard, who also owned the Toronto Maple Leafs. Ballard is a well-known talker, always traveling with the Leafs and making headlines.

"Vince Ferragamo is a hot item," I started out, "a great football player. Can you imagine what he will do for the Canadian Football League?"

Sazio and the accountant just looked at me.

"There were six hundred thousand empty seats in the league last year. With Vinnie playing for you, you'll fill them all!"

The accountant shifted in his chair, undoubtedly going through the numbers.

"But look what it will do for Hamilton." I talked to Sazio: If he could pull off such a deal, it would make him the top GM in the league—they'd all be beholden to him. "Vince will be what Pelé was for the Cosmos and soccer in America." I saw a little light of recognition in Sazio's eyes. "You know, the first game Pelé played for the Cosmos was at Randall's Island Stadium and the crowd was twenty-two thousand five-hundred. Pelé's last game was in Giants-Stadium, and the crowd was seventy-seven thousand."

"How much is this miracle man going to cost me?" Sazio asked.

Without blinking an eye: "Two million."

"Over how many years?"

"Four years. We can work out the exact terms if you people are serious."

"We're serious," Sazio said.

We kept on talking. Nothing concrete came from the meeting. Maybe they were serious, maybe not; but they hadn't turned me down or rejected the figure I was asking for. It didn't hurt to keep talking, and with every step I was getting a bigger toehold on some leverage to use against the Rams. I kept in touch with Sazio throughout December and January.

Vince played great ball that season. He threw 240 passes for 3,199 yards, passed for 30 touchdowns, and led the Rams to the play-offs. Those three statistics became a new Rams record, and they are a team that has known the likes of Norm van Brocklin and Bob Waterfield. Vince's completion percentage, at 59.7, was the best in the NFL. Statistically overall, he was second only to Ron Jaworski.

Vince was more certain than ever that a deal would be worked out. So was I. Why would the Rams let him go? But here we were in the middle of January. Vince would become a free agent on February 1, and, so far, not a word from the Rams.

I called Klosterman. His answer: "We'll get back to you."

I had to shake up Klosterman. First, I got Vince to be the main speaker and recipient at a Royal Canadian Legion sports dinner in Thunder Bay, Ontario. Immediately, rumors started circulating in Los Angeles that Vince was going to Canada.

And sure enough, I got a call from Klosterman. I flew to the Coast. Vince and I met Klosterman in his office at the Rams' training complex in Anaheim—an old elementary school the club had bought and converted.

Klosterman had taken the old principal's office and covered the walls with awards and plaques. He has a big desk and carpeted floors. He is a big guy, an ex-quarterback in the Canadian Football League, and he limps from a skiing accident suffered in Banff, near Calgary. A dear friend of Carroll Rosenbloom's, Klosterman had been in the Baltimore Colts' organization when Rosenbloom owned it. They went to the Coast together. Klosterman fitted well in Los Angeles; he bought a Mercedes 450 and a home in Beverly Hills. He knows everyone in football, in show business, in politics. The perfect GM, he can drop more names in a conversation than any man I've ever met.

Don knew football, and I was certain he knew Vince's value to the club. I told him that the Rams' previous offer to Vince was unsatisfactory.

"What *are* you looking for?" he asked me.

"A contract in excess of a million."

Don's forehead wrinkled. "We thought we had a deal with Caruso. We all agreed. I can't go in with those kinds of numbers. I'll never be able to convince *her*."

"Don, Vince was the number two passer. I'm not saying he should be the number one salaried quarterback. Let's say fourth best!"

Klosterman stretched his body halfway across the desk. "He doesn't deserve to be the highest-paid quarterback in the NFL."

"No one said *highest*. I said *fourth* best. Make it fifth best."

Klosterman sat back in his chair. Looking not the least bit concerned, not the least bit worried, he put his hands together in front of his face. "It's funny about football . . ." He paused, as if deep in thought, ". . .most players get their big money after they're over the hill, not while they're getting to the top."

I've heard this talk from every GM I have ever talked with. It just doesn't wash.

"Vince should be paid on the level of his performance, *now!*"

Seeing that the Rams were sitting tight, I turned to Vince and bit my lip. That was my signal to him. He picked himself up and said, "David, let's go."

I got up. Don didn't make a move. "David," he said, "take our offer. In time, Vince will work himself up the money ladder."

"Don, he's at the top of the performance ladder right now. His salary should match."

For a week nothing happened, and then a story—to this day no one knows how it got out—broke in the *L.A. Times*. It was reported that Harold Ballard was recently in Los Angeles with the Maple Leafs and had bumped into Vince Ferragamo on Hollywood Boulevard. The story said that Ballard was so impressed with Ferragamo that he was determined to lure him to Canada for the Tiger-Cats.

Instead of calling me, the Rams negotiated through the *Herald-*

Examiner. In the paper they said Vince was asking an outrageous salary of $360,000. Naturally, the Rams neglected to say what *they* were offering. Nor was there any mention of the terms.

The real problem with the Rams' offer in *any* amount was the deferred payment. They would keep a good bit of the money and pay it to Vince over the years.

Vince was popular in Los Angeles, and the Rams stories were hitting the papers in order to get their point across to their fans. Getting their side out first meant that no matter what we said, we would be on the defensive. It's very hard to win under those circumstances, and it was time to let everyone know that Vince did have somewhere else to go.

Vince, Jodi, and I flew to Canada the first week in February. When we got to Toronto International Airport, on our way to Thunder Bay, we were mobbed by reporters. A *Toronto Star* reporter, Rick Matsumoto, followed us all the way to Thunder Bay and wrote a major piece on Vince in the *Star*.

The trip to Thunder Bay was an experience. It takes a little under two hours in a small plane, but our plane carried cattle in the front section. Either the cattle were more valuable than the humans, or it was a question of weight distribution. In any case, the cattle flew first class, we were downwind.

Vince received an award at the dinner and lots of coverage. ABC sportscaster Dick Schaap, comedian Joe Mauro, and Montreal Expos All-Star catcher Gary Carter also were given awards. Carter got up and revealed the crazy turns that sports recruiting sometimes takes. He and Vince had gone to competitive high schools in Southern California. One weekend they were both being recruited by scouts from USC—Vince on a baseball scholarship, Carter as a quarterback. When we got back to Toronto, I made sure Vince and Jodi got to check out Hamilton. Their pictures were taken, the appropriate captions were attached, and the story was carried in the *L.A. Times* the next day. The Rams had to believe we were serious.

In Toronto I spoke with Sazio. He offered a $150,000-a-year contract—but only for one year. That was an insult, especially after Harold Ballard had implied in the *L.A. Times* that he was prepared to pay Vince $1.2 million over four years.

To find out how we could get Vince off Hamilton's negotiation

list, I immediately called the Canadian Football League Commissioner.

"There's no way you can do that," he said, "unless you make a
deal with another club."

We were stuck—or were we?

In this business you get a lot of ego-tripping show-offs—people
who'd call with a great deal for Vince. "Let's take a meeting at
Chasen's," they'd say. We would go; it was nothing. The "deal"
was a guy being seen with Vince Ferragamo. He had gotten his
jollies having people seeing him eat dinner with a celebrity.

Let's take one example of how people want to get into the act,
flatter themselves that they can make a deal for you. Back when
Vince was in New York shooting his Sasson Jeans commercial, we
had dinner at Oren and Aretsky: Vince, Jodi, Monica and I, Audrey Nizen, vice-president at Sasson Jeans, and Ed Hospadar,
who was then a New York Ranger but is now a defenseman for the
Hartford Whalers. Eddie, known as "the enforcer" for always getting into fights, invited us to a game the following week in Los
Angeles. He arranged with Jerry Buss, the millionaire bachelor
owner of the Forum, the Lakers, and the Los Angeles Kings, to
have us use his box between the benches as Jerry's guests.

It was the first game I'd ever been to where a waitress came to
take an order for mixed drinks. Jerry, known for his abundant
hospitality, put a welcome notice on the scoreboard: THE L. A.
KINGS WELCOME VINCE FERRAGAMO'S AGENT, DAVID
FISHOF, FROM NEW YORK.

During the game we sat with a friend of Jerry's who owns a
restaurant. Since I've forgotten his name, I'll call him the restaurateur. After the game we all went to Jerry's suite at the Forum,
where he was throwing a party for the many celebrities attending
the game. The restaurateur approached me and told me he could
get Vince the kind of contract we were looking for.

I was sure no one knew the figures we were asking for. "How?"
I asked him.

He told me that he and Georgia were good friends. "I play
tennis with her very often, two, three times a week. *In her
home.*" He also told me he'd introduce us to her psychiatrist, who
was coming to the party.

When the psychiatrist walked in, the restaurateur walked away without saying a word, without introducing us. Then the shrink told us we shouldn't believe a word the guy was saying. The psychiatrist saw Georgia all the time "in my office, on my couch," and since he was so close to her, he could get us the contract we want. He claimed that Georgia had been complaining to him weekly that because she was a woman and had just taken over the team, people were trying to take advantage of her.

"Are you ever by the Rams' training complex?" I asked him.

"Are you kidding? I'm there every week."

He agreed to meet with us the following Thursday and, of course, never showed up. I knew he was full of it. Had he really been Georgia's psychiatrist, he would never have told us who he was treating, let alone offer to act as a go-between.

Then there are the crackpot calls. Some seem sensible at first hearing, but later on you find they're all hot air. There are a lot of great ideas floating around, but there are very few people who want to spend the time and money, or have the intelligence, to make them work.

While I was in Thunder Bay, I got a call from a guy telling me I should get in touch with Nelson Skalbania. "Skalbania's buying a Canadian franchise. He's got a ton of money and wants Ferragamo to play for him. *Money's no object.*"

But if the caller had traced me all the way up here, it was worth a try. I called Skalbania.

"Yes, I'm buying a franchise," Skalbania said. "Montreal. But look, why don't you find out a little about who I am?"

I liked his approach: He didn't want to waste his or my time sparring around. Maybe this was a live one. I asked around. Skalbania was a Vancouver multimillionaire who'd been putting money into the sports field. He owned a couple of minor-league teams and a hockey club.

A week later I got a call from Skalbania. "David, I'm going to be in Montreal in two days. Why don't you come up? I'd like to talk to you."

At that time, Vince was at the Superstars, the ABC Sports Spectacular taking place in Key Biscayne. I wanted Vince with me to see how he and Skalbania would hit it off. Vince flew up to New York dressed in his jeans. I felt he should be better dressed to meet Skalbania; after all, we were talking millions. We went to see Tony Sciametta, a vice-president in a Wall Street foreign-exchange house. Tony had a tailor come up to his office, and Vince was outfitted in a couple of hours.

We had to be careful. Newspaper people are always checking airline reservations to catch a lead; so we went to Montreal under assumed names. We arrived at night and went straight to the hotel and to bed.

The next morning we went out and walked around to get a feel of the place, talking to everyone we met—waitresses, newspaper dealers, several taxi drivers—asking them about the Alouettes. We also heard rumors that Vince Ferragamo was going to play in the Canadian league. All these people were talking to us about Vince, and nobody realized they were talking *to* him.

We met Skalbania at his enormous suite at the Four Seasons. Vince and I sat at each end of a big down sofa in the living room. Flowers were everywhere, with fruit on the table and champagne in several ice buckets. That's the image Skalbania likes to project. Nothing wrong with it—when you've got it, flaunt it.

Skalbania was across from us, sitting in the middle of an equally large, soft sofa. He had his feet up on the glass table between us. At the time he was 42 but looked a lot younger. He has a rich, healthy look: tall, thin, tan. He's a wheeler-dealer who habitually speaks quickly:

"You know, I own the Calgary Flames of the NHL."

"I know you moved the club from Atlanta to Calgary," I replied. "Very smart," I added.

He took his feet off the table and sat up. "Smart?" A smile crossed his face, and he leaned forward. "Let me tell you. The Atlanta franchise was on the market. I heard that a couple of guys in Canada were bidding on it. I outbid them. I went in with sixteen million dollars—U.S. dollars. Top money." As he talked, Skalbania sat a little taller. "I got it: one million in thirty days, nine million in sixty days, six million in ninety days."

"A lot of money for a club in Calgary," I said to stroke him.

"Yeah." He smiled again. "But listen to this." The smile turned into the smirk of the cat that caught the canary. "I put up my million. No sweat!" He waved a hand in the air. "The contract is mine. Then I go to the guys up here who were bidding against me for the team and I offer them forty-nine percent for ten million dollars."

Now I smiled. He was about to tell me how he'd screwed them—but he had also told me how I could deal with *him*.

Skalbania accepted my smile as a compliment. "No, no. Wait, there's more. They go for the ten. So I got my million back, and I cover the nine million in sixty days."

"And the other six million?"

Skalbania laughed. "It's a beauty. I go to the local Calgary TV station and sell them the rights to broadcast the games there for a couple of years. They grab at it and pay me six million."

Not bad. He ended up with 51 percent of the team, and it hadn't cost him a dime.

He went on, wanting to show us what a great deal maker he is. Proud of his achievements, he told us about his real estate deals, his oil deals. "Everything I touch turns to gold."

I nodded approvingly. Fine, we're listening, we're duly impressed. He's in the big leagues, we're in the big leagues. We'll talk to him at his level.

He asked us, "What do you want?"

"Two and a half million dollars in salary plus a piece of the gate."

"One million," Skalbania retorted.

I remembered that Skalbania had told the newspapers and his friends that he was going to sign Ferragamo. Why should I budge? He'd already committed himself.

"No," I said firmly. "This is Vince's price. Two and a half plus a percentage."

We went back and forth, and we finally agreed on $2.5 million in salary. I felt that it wasn't over yet.

Skalbania sat down again across from us and started telling me what a beautiful stadium they have in Montreal. "Olympic Stadium—sixty thousand seats. It's the biggest football stadium in Canada, and Vinnie over here is going to fill it."

I was listening carefully: It sounded like the same story I had fed Sazio. Maybe they'd talked together?

Skalbania went on and on, selling himself, working himself into a sweat. I just kept on agreeing with him, nodding my head, sipping my champagne, and working the numbers in my head. I was still after a percentage of the gate. Finally I interrupted: "How many people normally come to a game?" I knew the figure was twenty thousand.

"Twenty-five thousand to thirty thousand. But with Vinnie"— Skalbania looked toward Vince and winked—"we're going to fill it to the brim." Skalbania's eyes were gleaming. He was out to capture Montreal and become a Canadian Steinbrenner.

"Look," I said, putting my glass on the table and leaning forward, "if you have twenty thousand people now and Vince comes to Montreal, you're going to get sixty-five thousand every game."

"Yeah!" Skalbania answered quickly, proud of what he was going to accomplish.

"That means that Vince is drawing forty thousand people. *Forty thousand!*" I repeated. "You're talking ten games at forty thousand people at an extra ten dollars a seat."

Suddenly Skalbania's body became very still. He just looked at me.

"That's four million dollars you're making on Vince Ferragamo."

"But look at the salary I'm paying him."

I turn to Vince and frowned. "Six hundred twenty-five thousand dollars a season and you're making four million *extra* on him. I don't think that's fair."

Before we went in, Vince and I had agreed that no matter what he thought—whether he agreed with me or disagreed—he would say *nothing* during the negotiations. That way, we always had an out. And again, you have to remember, this was all for leverage— or so we thought. Vince picked up on my signal, nodded his head, put his glass on the table, and started to get up.

"Wait!" Skalbania said, jumped up, and came around. He sat down next to Vince, placing a hand on his shoulder to keep him on the couch. Skalbania had been counting on announcing his acquisition of the Montreal Alouettes and getting one of the NFL's best quarterbacks at the same time. He wanted to shock Montreal, and Vince was essential to his PR.

"What do *you* want?" he asked Vince.

"Talk to David," Vince said, pointing at me.

Skalbania turned around. I got up and started walking around the sofa so as to get behind Skalbania. "Let's say the normal attendance is thirty thousand . . . thirty thousand." I was letting him know I was accepting the figure he quoted. "Vince must get twenty-five percent of the gross difference between thirty and sixty thousand people."

Skalbania turned his head and looked at me. "Ticket dollars?"

I leaned over the sofa and looked directly at him. "Yep. Ticket dollars. And the way we do this is that after every game, we keep all the rip-off parts of the tickets. We line up all the stubs and know the *real* attendance."

Skalbania agreed to allow me to examine box-office receipts after every game. All he saw was himself announcing his twin coups (buying the Alouettes and signing Ferragamo) in front of the cameras, on the front pages of every Canadian newspaper. He was establishing an image of himself across Canada and didn't care how much it would cost. Later on he would discover that the city of Montreal takes 25 percent of the gross receipts for taxes and rent. Without realizing it, he had put himself in a hole.

Theoretically I'd gotten Vince the best quarterback deal in all of football. I was satisfied, Vince was satisfied. There was nothing on paper, but all the time we were thinking this was merely an exercise—since we really wanted to play in Los Angeles. It was a great deal, but I made sure to spell it out very carefully for Skalbania: *This is the deal if Vince decides to play football in Canada.*

We shook hands on it. Everything had to stay a secret. "Especially," I told Skalbania, "don't say anything to Bob Geary," who was the Alouettes' GM. I knew of Geary's friendship with Klosterman. They had played football together in Canada, and I didn't want Klosterman to know we had made a deal in Canada only because Vince really wanted to play in L.A.

For my part, I was happy it all remained buried. The guy I had made a deal with didn't own a ball club, but I had my leverage.

I went back to the States expecting to deal with the Rams, but they weren't the least bit interested in talking. As far as they were concerned, they had Vince on the short end of the stick and wanted to keep him there.

I told them there was a deal in Canada and mentioned the Alouettes. "If you want Vince to play for the Rams next year," I said, "we'd better start talking."

I believed Klosterman and Geary had been talking, but that Geary knew nothing of the deal I had made with Skalbania. So, of course, Klosterman didn't believe me. He was in no rush. All he said was: "We'll get back to you." It was becoming the Rams' standard statement to me.

What was strange was that Vince is the second-best quarterback on record in the NFL *and a free agent*, and I didn't hear from any teams wanting him. It began to smack of collusion, a violation of the antitrust statutes. As if they had been reading my mind, suddenly both Green Bay (Wisconsin) and St. Louis called me. Saint Louis never called back, but I did talk with Bob Harland, general manager at Green Bay. He offered $125,000, $150,000, and $175,000—a three-year contract.

"Are you serious?" I asked.

"That's double the salary he's getting now," remarked Harland.

I couldn't resist telling him, "Bob, that's enough for me. What are you going to pay Vince for throwing the football?" Vince was being sandbagged. If we accepted the Green Bay Packers' offer, the Rams would match it, and Vince would have to play for much less than he deserved. The Canadian deal looked better and better.

Actually, as a straight money deal, it was tremendous, even historic. At that time, no professional ballplayer was getting a piece of the gate. It has happened since, but we initiated it.

As the Canadian story started to leak (with Skalbania sending it out, of course), I got a phone call from Brent Musburger of CBS sports. "Hey, Big Guy. Let's go to L.A. tomorrow and do an interview with Skalbania, Klosterman, and you."

Skalbania had now officially purchased the Alouettes. But Vince had not signed with him, and Skalbania was in California running after Vince to sign.

I called Skalbania at the Beverly Hills Hotel, and he agreed to have an interview with Brent and me the next day. Brent picked me up in his limo and we flew to L.A. It had to be one of my funniest trips, because I didn't stop laughing from New York to California. Brent's producer was with him; they had a file of my press clippings, so he knew my whole life story. Since his name was Musburger, I believed he also was Jewish, so I told him Jewish jokes the whole trip. And I know plenty of them from all those years in the Catskills. As it turned out, Musburger is not Jewish and didn't understand a word I was saying, but he led me on, laughing when I laughed. This went on until the plane was touching down in L.A., when he announced, "David, I'm a goy."

A limo picked us up, and we headed to the CBS studios in Hollywood, where Brent had to tape his daily radio show. I didn't want a lot of hassling with phone calls, so I consented to the interview only as long as no one knew I was in town. Even then I was a little concerned about going with Brent to the CBS studios.

"Don't worry, Big Guy," said Musburger. "No one will recognize you. You go into an office, make the calls you have to, and I'll do the radio show. We'll be out of here in thirty minutes."

When I walked into the studio, there was a big sign on the blackboard: IF VINCE FERRAGAMO SIGNS WITH CANADA, YOU CAN REACH HIS AGENT, DAVID FICHOFF, AT THE FOUR SEASONS IN MONTREAL OR HIS HOME PHONE NUMBER . . .

I panicked and told Brent, "Let me out of here." But before I could make a move, in walked Jim Hill, a local CBS sportscaster and a former Rams player. "Do you know this David Fichoff guy?" he asked Brent. "He doesn't return my calls. I can't find out what's going on with Ferragamo."

I found an empty office and made my phone calls, afraid that at any minute someone would realize I was there and the whole studio would come storming in. But it didn't happen. Brent finished his show, came to get me, and told me to go into the limo. On his way out, he wrote on the blackboard: "Sorry, guys, you just missed him. And he spells his name FISHOF."

At the interview, Brent asked the all-important question: "What's the difference between the Rams' offer and Montreal?"

"Millions" was my answer.

In Los Angeles the atmosphere was heating up. With Skalbania there and Musburger around, people were beginning to talk. The week before, Vince had his own tennis tournament with Rod

Carew to benefit the mentally retarded. The tournament was arranged by Mario Dalessi, a board member of the California Angels and general manager of the Jolly Roger Inn in Anaheim, California. Many of the Rams players took part in the tournament and hinted to Vince that they didn't want him to leave. Vince called me and said he wanted to reconsider.

With Skalbania in Los Angeles, Klosterman got nervous. Suddenly he began thinking there might be truth to what I had been telling him. He asked for a meeting, and this time I brought our attorney, Ed Barton, along with me. Barton, a lawyer with Pacht, Ross, Warne, Bernhard, and Sears, was preparing the technical language of the contract.

We met Klosterman in a room on the second floor of a two-story Anaheim motel. Klosterman didn't holler or yell, but he advised us against the Canadian deal. His tone was confidential: Vince's style of playing football would not fit in with the way they play in Canada. What he wanted was another chance to go back to Georgia Frontiere with an offer. He didn't want to talk numbers. He wanted to know only if we were still interested in playing in L.A.

We told him we were, and that we were going to Vince's house and wait for his phone call. If they were serious, we'd talk numbers.

Klosterman called back with an offer of $1.3 million. The problem once again was that most of the money was to be deferred, paid out over many years. Vince would not be getting very much now, and certainly nowhere near the Canadian deal. It was the Rams' final offer.

Vince didn't like it, declined the offer, and took off with Jodi for Omaha and a visit with his in-laws.

When he got back, he wanted to take the Rams' offer. It was Passover. Vince knew I didn't like to work on a Jewish holiday, so he phoned Ed Barton. Then, on his own, Vince called Klosterman and told him that he would accept the original Ram offer.

The Rams sent contracts to Barton's office. I believed Vince wanted to play in L.A. so badly he would have signed the contracts. Then suddenly, two hours later, John Shaw, vice-president, called Barton: The Rams were no longer interested in signing Ferragamo!

When I found out what had happened, I asked John Shaw to keep it quiet because I didn't want to lose my leverage in Canada. If Skalbania knew the Rams were no longer interested in Ferragamo, he would probably offer us less money and we would be in a corner with nowhere else to go. I quickly made arrangements with Skalbania to call a press conference and have Vince sign.

Then the phones started ringing off the hook. For the last days of Passover, I went with Monica and Shira to my parents' home. By the end of April, the Canadian deal was wrapped up. Vince had signed, and the story was big news when it hit the papers.

Out in Los Angeles, there was a lot of handwringing and recrimination. They claimed that Vince was "deserting" the Rams, that he had "defected to Canada." They depicted Vince as the runaway quarterback, as if it was his fault that he wasn't playing in Los Angeles. Nonsense! We were always ready and willing to deal with the Rams. Not believing we had an option, the Rams never came in with a legitimate offer. They knew Vince wanted to play football and were sure he was locked in as a free agent. If he wanted to play, he would play for them *on their terms*.

What made it so odd was the irrationality of it all. If the Rams had another quarterback, that would have been something else. But they had no one else, and they weren't looking, either!

Vince went off to Canada, but he didn't have a good year. There were a lot of problems right from the start. To begin with, I felt there was a lot of jealousy on the part of the coach, Joe Scanello. During the season Scanello walked into the GM's office and said to Bob Geary, "How can the players have a guaranteed salary and make more money than me?"

Vince came in with a lot of media play—newspaper articles and TV interviews. In an attempt to soothe the players, the Alouettes gave each one a $5,000 salary increase. But still, that was nowhere near the kind of money Vince was getting.

Then there was the style of Canadian football. There are twelve players on each team, the field is larger, and, most important, a quarterback has to do a lot of running. Vince hadn't been a scrambler since his college days. In Los Angeles he was used to a great offensive line protecting him—men like Dennis Harrah, Doug France, Jack Slater, and Rich Saul. Now he had to learn a whole new style of play. Unfortunately, there wasn't much time and the coaching staff wasn't much help. As Vince told me one night over the phone, "It's like Skalbania bought a million-dollar computer and then hired people at two dollars an hour to run it."

Once the season got under way, it became obvious the Alouettes had a superstar with nothing around him. The Canadian media and the Montreal fans turned hostile as the Alouettes lost game after game. Sportswriters, who had previously hyped the coming of a new era in Canadian football, now began questioning Skalbania's judgment, not only in buying and running the team, but in acquiring Ferragamo and the other Americans—James Scott, David Overstreet, Keith Gary, and Billy "White Shoes" Johnson. The Alouettes had a miserable season, winning three games while losing thirteen.

The Rams' season didn't prove much better; they won six games and lost ten. They wound up carrying Dan Pastorini, Pat Haden, Jeff Rudledge, and Congressman Jack Kemp's son, Jack, Jr. as quarterbacks—which cost them in excess of $600,000. They could have had Vince for half that money.

I was in and out of Los Angeles on other business, but occasionally I bumped into Don Klosterman and we would "unofficially" discuss the possibility of Vince coming back to the Rams. It was all talk. Klosterman couldn't do anything by himself. Georgia Frontiere owned the team and it would be her decision if Vince were to return. Besides, Klosterman or the Rams couldn't really discuss Vince; he was the property of the Alouettes and they would need the Alouettes' permission to enter into negotiations.

I had been hearing stories that Skalbania was in financial trouble and looking to sell the team. George Allen and Bill Harris, a real estate developer, were heading a group that was talking about buying the Alouettes. So it was not surprising that in December, while I was in San Francisco to watch the 49ers-Giants game in the play-offs, I got a call from Skalbania. He was in Palm Springs and wanted to come up to San Francisco to meet me.

We got together at the San Francisco airport. His wife was with him, and the three of us sat down to talk about Vince. Skalbania wanted out of the contract.

"Fine," I said. "You can buy out the contract for one million dollars."

"No way, David."

"One million," I repeated.

His wife joined in. "We haven't any money. We're broke," she said, her voice rising. "What do you want from us?"

I looked at her. She was dressed beautifully, very expensively, with lots of jewelry, diamonds and gold. "I don't want anything from you that's not in the contract. We have a deal."

"But we don't have any money." Her voice was shrill.

I turned to Skalbania. He had a hangdog expression on his face, his eyes were sad; he seemed to have aged ten years since I last saw him. Perhaps he was having a hard time, but all I could think of was that here was a man who had just flown in from Palm Springs, one of the most exclusive areas of the world, reserved not for the rich but for the super rich, and he had flown in with his own plane. How bad off could he be?

"Look, Nelson," I said, "you don't want Vince to come up to Canada? Okay. Vince's contract right now is worth approximately two million dollars. And I'm not talking about the percentage of the gate. I'm talking straight salary. I'll take fifty cents on the dollar."

"David," Skalbania said in a very quiet voice, "there's a guy in Los Angeles, Harry Ornest, who will negotiate this for me. I won't pay you a million, but I want to settle this. Give Harry a call, see him and work something out."

I decided to stay a few days on the Coast and see what could be done. After the 49ers game I flew to Los Angeles, checked into the Century Plaza Hotel, and called Ornest.

"Ah, David," he said, "Nelson told me all about you. Let's have dinner tonight."

"That's very kind of you," I said, "but I really have to get back to New York as soon as possible. Can we just meet and talk?"

"Sure, we'll talk. Sure we'll talk," Ornest was bubbling friendliness over the phone. "But you're in Los Angeles. Let's have dinner."

What could I do? I agreed to have dinner with him, and he asked me to meet him in front of the hotel at 8:00 P.M.

At eight o'clock I was standing at the hotel entrance when I saw an old Rambler drive up. A woman sitting in the passenger seat was waving at me. I didn't know her. "David," she called. I walked over to the car, not really believing this was Ornest's car. I had made several phone calls from San Francisco and had learned Ornest was a wealthy man; he had made his money when he sold Skalbania the Vancouver triple-A baseball team.

"David, so nice to meet you," the lady in the Rambler said and introduced herself as Mrs. Ornest. He was sitting in the driver's seat. I got into the back of the car and shook hands with him.

"Where are we going?" I asked as Ornest took off immediately.

"R.J.'s."

"R.J.'s?" I couldn't believe it. Fred Dryer introduced me to R.J.'s. It's one of my favorite spots in Beverly Hills. "How can we talk in R.J.'s?" I asked, wondering how I was going to negotiate with Ornest while his wife was there. "R.J.'s is so noisy. And there's always people coming by saying hello." Even as I said this, I realized that was exactly why he had picked R.J.'s.

"Don't worry," Ornest said. "We'll get a quiet corner table. Besides, my sons are planning to meet us there."

"Oh." This guy was full of surprises. "How come?"

"Well, one of my sons plays baseball and since you represent Lou Piniella, I want you to meet him. My other son is going to be a general manager one day and he should see what a negotiation is all about."

There was no need to answer that. I just sat back and let him drive. We got to R.J.'s and it was packed. Ornest made sure to say hello to everyone he knew and introduced me as Vince Ferragamo's agent. I saw people I knew and I had to go over and talk to them. It was exactly what I didn't want. We finally sat down, and I wanted to start talking business right away, but Ornest wanted a drink first, and then his sons arrived and we were one big, happy family.

Finally Ornest said to me: "David, Nelson has no money."

"Well, it's not going to cost him much to buy out Vince's contract," I said.

"Good!" Ornest's face broke out into a big smile. "So, we can do some business together?"

"Absolutely, Harry. You and I will work out a deal."

"Terrific."

I leaned close to him and said, "He can buy the contract for a million dollars."

The smile immediately disappeared from Ornest's face. His

eyes hardened. He moved away from me. "You have to be kidding!"

"No," I said. "One million dollars."

Ornest flared up; he got angry. Maybe because his wife and sons were sitting there listening and he couldn't move me. Maybe because Skalbania still owed him a lot of money and they had worked out a deal if Ornest could get Skalbania off the hook. Whatever, he started shouting: "You should pay us to get Vince out of the contract."

"Harry," I said as gently as I could, "I can't negotiate here in this restaurant." I got up. "You stay. Enjoy your meal. I'll give Nelson a call tomorrow." And I left the restaurant and went to bed.

I spoke with Skalbania, and he agreed to meet me in Los Angeles at the Bel-Air Hotel in two weeks. On the appointed day Vince and I were going through the lobby and saw Bill Harris talking on the phone. He called us over and said to Vince, "Say hello to George."

Vince got on the phone and spoke to George Allen, who tried to convince Vince that they should get together. George wanted to buy the Alouettes, and the biggest stumbling block was Vince's contract; his salary and percentage of the gate were too much of a burden.

When we got up to Skalbania's suite, we found him eager to buy out the contract so he could sell the club without a new owner assuming Vince's contract, while, on the other hand, he didn't want to pay the money we were asking for. I believe Skalbania's biggest problem was that he was listening to Harry Ornest, who had been promising him he would get rid of Ferragamo cheap by intimidating him in private and public. Ornest had been constantly calling Vince's father and then had gone after a *Los Angeles Times* reporter with information about Vince's contract and his alleged tax problems with the Canadian government.

Skalbania wanted to sell the team, and so we eventually were able to reach an agreement on a buy-out. We settled for $750,000. We even agreed to Skalbania's desire to make the money payable over a two-year period. That was fine with us; we wanted out of the contract so we could start serious negotiations with the Rams. We shook hands and Skalbania said, "Write it up, have your lawyer look it over and send it to me."

After our meeting, we went to Ed Barton's office. He wrote up an agreement and sent it over to Skalbania. A couple of weeks went by and I still hadn't gotten it back, signed by Skalbania. I called him. He told me he was just going to get in touch. No, not about the agreement, that was still with his lawyer, but it would be okay, we shouldn't worry about it. What he wanted was for Vince to go to Hawaii. Skalbania was scheduled to give a talk at some exclusive millionaires' club about how he made a fortune in sports. He wanted Vince to walk in while he was talking, pick up a football, and throw it to Skalbania, who would catch it. Then Vince would take Skalbania's place at the speaker's stand and talk about the differences between United States and Canadian football. Skalbania offered to pay all of Vince's expenses—he could bring Jodi with him—and Skalbania would throw in a thousand dollars.

Vince went to Hawaii, but then a week later he got the check back marked "insufficient funds." We called Skalbania, and he wired the money directly into Vince's bank account, but I read the bounced check as a danger signal. And sure enough, on March 1 there was no payment of the $100,000 that the Alouettes owed Vince as part of his salary.

I called Skalbania. He claimed they had to hold on to the money because of tax payments Vince owed the Canadian government.

"That's not true, Nelson. Vince has worked out an arrangement for his taxes with the Canadian government and his tax status has nothing to do with the Alouettes."

Skalbania insisted he was holding the money until he had clearance from the Canadian tax bureau, but I was certain it was either a way for Skalbania not to pay Vince his money or, worse, he didn't have the money to pay it.

I immediately called Ed Barton and asked him to send the Alouettes a letter that they were in default of their contract with Vince and that either they pay the money or send us a letter giving Vince permission to seek employment in the NFL—a letter we needed to avoid charges of "tampering."

Now I had two problems in reopening negotiations. First, I had to make a deal before anyone found out the Alouettes were in default; I couldn't let it be known that Vince might not have a job if the team went bankrupt. Second, I had to make a deal before the football draft, which was only a month away.

So I called Klosterman and we had an "unofficial" meeting in his home in Hollywood Hills. We sat in his library and talked. "Look, Don. What do you want to do with Vince? I know you need him."

I was talking not just about the Rams but about Klosterman himself. There was a power struggle going on inside the Rams' organization between Klosterman and Jack Faulkner, the administrator of football operations, and the coach, Ray Malavasi. The Rams had lost a lot of top players: Vince, Jack Reynolds, Fred Dryer, and Bob Brudzinski. They had had a terrible year. Their draft prospects for 1982 didn't look good at all. Klosterman had been pressing Georgia Frontiere to reopen talks to get Vince back. Faulkner and Malavasi wanted Bert Jones, who had filed for free agency from Baltimore and had expressed a desire to play in Los Angeles.

The question of who would be the next quarterback for the Rams had nothing to do with who would be good for the team, but which faction won out. My personal feeling was that Faulkner and Malavasi both liked Vince, but because Klosterman was for Vince, they took the other side and opted for Jones, who they believed Georgia Frontiere wanted.

Georgia played it smart. She allowed Faulkner to go after Jones, and Klosterman to start talking with me.

So now I was sitting with Don trying to work out a deal. "For Vince to come back we have to have a minimum of three hundred thousand dollars a year."

"That's impossible, David. All I can do is bring back the last offer that was on the table."

"Which was?" I asked, knowing its contents full well.

"Four years, starting at a hundred fifty thousand dollars and going to two hundred twenty-five thousand; a total package of seven hundred fifty thousand dollars."

"I can't take that."

"I can't make a deal for any more."

"That's up to you," I said. "But why don't you talk to Georgia. I'll stay in town a few days. Give me a call."

Rumors were flying around Los Angeles as to who the next quarterback of the Rams would be, Jones or Ferragamo. At the same time, we finally got Bob Geary, the Alouettes' general manager, to send a letter to the Rams giving them permission to talk to Vince or his agent. A meeting was set up—officially now—at John Shaw's house. John Shaw is the vice-president of the Rams. I had first met John when he was sitting in on negotiations with Klosterman during my initial talks with the team. I felt John had been there to help balance their side in numbers; it was two against two.

First, the meeting was called for Wednesday, then postponed to Thursday, then Friday. Finally I said, "Saturday night is the latest I can wait."

I felt the Rams kept postponing the meeting, although they denied it, because they were waiting for an arbitrator's decision on a contract dispute between Jones and Robert Irsay, the Baltimore Colts' owner. A decision had been expected at any moment. Now it appeared that it would be awhile before anything was announced, so we finally sat down on Saturday night.

With me were Marvin Sears and Ed Barton. The other side had John Shaw and Don Klosterman. Shaw and Klosterman knew Marvin because he is the attorney for the Rams' team physician, Dr. Robert Kerlan.

"What we want," I started, "is a five-year contract starting at three hundred thousand dollars and going to five hundred thousand."

"Let's not worry about the length of the contract first," Klosterman said. "Let's talk about the amounts."

"No," I said. "Let's talk five years, *guaranteed*." We were very insistent on playing in L.A. Vince wanted to play in his hometown. He was certain he could play better near his family, in front of his friends. We were also concerned that once the Rams signed him—if they got Jones—they would trade him away. So, we were demanding a no-trade clause.

"We can't give you that," Klosterman said to us. "But you fellows have my word: We have no intention of trading Vince."

"Really?" Sears asked, his voice rising to convey his skepticism.

"Absolutely!" Klosterman said, looking from Sears to Barton to me.

"Then why not put it in the contract?" I asked.

"We can't do that because all the other players will start asking for it." He paused, then added, "But you can trust me."

We never got to the actual amounts of money, because we could not settle on the terms of the contract and the no-trade clause. At one point, we offered a concession: There wouldn't have to be a no-trade clause, but if Vince was traded he would get an extra $100,000. (In a sense, we were asking them to put their money where their mouths were.) But they wouldn't agree to that either, and so the meeting broke up.

I was convinced the Rams were still interested in Vince, so I called John Shaw two days later and asked if we could meet privately. John and I had developed a mutual respect for each other, and I felt that just the two of us, alone, could work something out.

And we did. In half an hour John and I settled on a five-year contract, starting at $300,000 with increases to $500,000 over the five-year period. I did not get the no-trade clause, but I had a terrific deal. We shook hands on it with the understanding that it had to remain absolutely quiet and that the agreement must be approved by Vince and Georgia Frontiere.

John assured me that there were no hard feelings on Georgia's part toward Vince; she did not feel vindictive because of his leaving; and the reason she wanted Jones was that her "football advisers" were telling her Jones was a better quarterback.

I've always wondered if they were the same advisers who told her to get rid of Jack Reynolds, allowing him to go to the Super Bowl with the 49ers in 1982. Undoubtedly they were the same advisers who told her she didn't need Bob Brudzinski. She got rid of him, and he went to the Miami Dolphins and the Super Bowl in 1983.

We added a proviso as we continued talking. If the Rams did sign Jones, or any other first-string quarterback, I would have the right to go out and make a deal for Vince with any club. I needed this because I felt Vince was worth more to any other club, and that we had settled with the Rams because Vince wanted to stay in Los Angeles. He took less money in order to stay in his hometown, and it would be unfair to trade him away *at that salary* to another club.

After the meeting I went straight to Vince's house and explained the deal to him and Jodi. Vince was bothered by the possibility of being traded away. He couldn't see himself as anything but a Ram.

So we accepted the deal. I called John Shaw. He said he'd spoken to Georgia and that she was thinking it over. However, she had several new conditions she wanted. First, I could go out and negotiate with any team but a West Coast club. I suspect she didn't want us going to the Raiders, with whom she was in a legal battle about their coming to Los Angeles. Second, no word of the negotiations must get into the media. I was all for that myself. Third, I could not discuss any of the negotiations with any other Ram officials. I hedged on this one. I had picked up enough information to know that Vince was being squeezed between the two factions vying for power in the Rams' organization. Georgia had asked Klosterman to sound out the other clubs, looking to trade Vince for draft picks. It was only later that I found out that she had given John Shaw the job of negotiating a contract for Vince, while, at the same time, she gave Klosterman the job of trading him away.

I called John when I found out. I was angry because we had agreed at our last meeting what the compensation would be if I made a deal with a new team. I needed this agreement so I could deal freely; now suddenly I found myself competing against Klosterman.

After repeated calls to Klosterman, I finally got to talk to him. "I'm trying to get the best deal for Vinnie," he said. For Vinnie, my foot! Klosterman rightly suspected he was losing his position of influence and, in order to prove his worth to Georgia, was looking for a sensational deal, *one that would benefit him.*

While I was free to go out and negotiate, there was little I could do since few teams would talk seriously with me. They were waiting to see what Klosterman would trade for. The Chicago Bears, however, were very interested in Vince, and were willing to talk. Jim Finks, the Bears' general manager told me, "David, George Halas wants Ferragamo. And don't worry about the money. He'll pay it."

"You know about Klosterman looking for draft picks?"

"Of course," Finks said.

"What would you give him for Vince?"

"A second round."

I called Klosterman. "Don, you owe me one."

"About what?"

"I know you're trying to trade Vince. The Bears are interested. We can work something out. They'll take a second round for Vince."

Klosterman laughed. "Not enough, David. I want two number ones."

It was totally unrealistic in the NFL. Klosterman wasn't negotiating for Vince. He was looking to keep his job.

I was on the phone between Chicago and Los Angeles every day. I kept telling Klosterman what Halas would do, and Don kept telling me he could make a better deal. We were negotiating right down to the wire. Then, the night before the draft, it all came apart. The Rams picked up Bert Jones from Baltimore, giving up a first- and second-round selection. Now the Rams had a first-string quarterback, but had lost two good draft picks. They were planning to trade Vince for what they had lost in acquiring Jones. Chicago was ready to deal, but the Rams never called. Jim Finks stayed up till midnight waiting for the call; it never came.

Things were quiet after the draft and then began picking up in the beginning of May. Skalbania appointed Ornest governor of the Alouettes to sort out the club's financial problems. One of those problems was Vince's contract. Ornest's strategy was to try to convince the NFL teams that if they wanted to sign Vince Ferragamo, then they had to deal with him because he claimed Vince had a "personal-service" contract with Skalbania, which he now controlled. What Ornest didn't understand was that the personal-service contract was to *play* football, not *be* a football for Ornest to use in making a name for himself. Ornest was going around saying he owned Ferragamo.

How could he own him? Vince's contract was to play football for the Alouettes. The Alouettes didn't exist; the team was bankrupt. I kept telling the Bears, who were still interested in Vince, that Ornest had nothing to do with Vince's contract, but I suspect they were scared by his tactics.

In the middle of May, I got a call from Howard Cosell. He wanted Vince to be on his ABC *Sportsbeat* show. I complained to Howard about the treatment Vince had received when he went to Canada; Howard and other sportswriters used words like "deserted" and "ran away" as if Vince were a coward and were fleeing America.

Howard agreed with me that the press was unfair and asked me to see him. I went to his office at ABC. He sat me down and said, "I want to help Vince. He's a good quarterback without a team. I like him. I feel he's been wrongly treated and I want to give him a hearing."

Terrific! I agreed to have Vince appear on the show and he flew in to New York; together we went to Howard's apartment the Saturday night before the show. I wanted Cosell to see what was in the contract. Howard, being an attorney, would know how to read it and make the appropriate interpretations. Cosell had just flown in from the Kentucky Derby, so we didn't meet till late at night.

Cosell's producer, Ed Silverman, was with him. I was still concerned about the way Howard would handle Vince. Cosell is a very powerful figure on the American sports scene, especially in football, where he is close friends with many of the owners. They would be watching and listening to his show, and I had to be sure Vince was treated fairly.

Howard insisted he wanted to bring all the facts to light: "An injustice has been done and I want to help correct it," was what he said.

The show was taped early Sunday morning and aired that afternoon. The next day the papers in Los Angeles were running the story. It required some response from the Rams. Now, while suddenly admitting we had been talking, they claimed that there had not been any written agreement and that they couldn't really talk officially because of Vince's uncertain status in the Canadian Football League.

I read this as a signal: Get clearance from the Canadian Football League and we'll talk with you.

We already had permission from the Alouettes, but the team no longer existed. The George Allen-Bill Harris deal to buy the Alouettes had fallen through. The Alouettes had gone into bankruptcy, and the league had given the Montreal franchise to Charles Bronfman, who owned the Montreal Expos. Bronfman changed the name of the Alouettes to the Concordes and picked up the contracts of all the players, *except Vince Ferragamo and a lineman, Larry Pfohl.*

I protested this illegal action to the CFL Players Association; if Bronfman had the franchise, then he had to be responsible for *all* the old contracts. (I happened to meet Bronfman at a Hebrew University dinner honoring Bowie Kuhn. Bronfman admitted to me that the only reason he bought the club was that he had assurances he would not be responsible for Ferragamo's contract.) The Players Association said they would back us up; Vince was under contract to the team. If the team was sold, the new owner had to assume all the contracts. But when push came to shove, the Players Association did nothing. They weren't going to let a whole team go down because of one player, and certainly not because of Vince Ferragamo.

I then called Jake Gaudaur, the Commissioner of the CFL. He told me Vince was under a personal-service contract to Skalbania and not to the Montreal Alouettes, so the Concordes did not have to pick up his contract. It was nonsense! I had been lied to by the CFL Commissioner.

We were going around in circles. Vince wasn't wanted on the team in Canada, and we couldn't get a release from the CFL so we could negotiate a contract with the NFL. They were playing games with Vince's career.

I contacted Jay Moyer, the NFL's legal counsel. He told me he needed a letter affirming the default of the Alouettes' contract with Vince. Jay asked for whatever correspondence I had had with the CFL Commissioner and for copies of the contract with the Alouettes. Jay sent a letter to Skalbania, with a copy to Ornest, asking him if he did have a personal-service contract with Vince and/or if Skalbania had *any claims against Vince Ferragamo.* The letter also stated that if there were any claims, they had to be listed and verified. The NFL asked for a reply in seven days.

At that time, Skalbania was in Hong Kong at the Mandarin Hotel. Word from his secretary was that he was out trying to raise some money. Ornest did answer the letter. He said they had claims against Vince, but he didn't list them.

May stretched into June; suddenly it was the first week of July and nothing was happening. I spoke with Jay Moyer again. He understood what was going on and thought it was unfair to Vince. He spoke with Commissioner Pete Rozelle, who looked over the correspondence, the contracts, and what had been happening, and sent the following wire to the Rams:

> This office has received no explanation from Mr. Skalbania or Mr. Ornest of the basis for any claim that Vince Ferragamo is not currently free to sign in the NFL for the 1982 season and beyond, nor even a clear indication that such a claim is in fact being asserted. In these circumstances, and without purporting to decide the merits of any such claim, this office is in no position to preclude Vince Ferragamo and the L.A. Rams from negotiating and executing one or more NFL player contracts . . .

That opened the door. I flew to California and in a meeting with John Shaw and Vince at the Jolly Roger Inn, we worked out a new deal. This one actually turned out better than the old one we had shaken hands on three months earlier. The money was the same—a little over a million dollars—but now it was spaced over three years rather than five.

Vince was once again a Ram, and once again his luck at coming out a winner held. Jones was slated as the first-string quarterback, and everyone was sure Vince would be traded. But in the fourth game of the season, right after the strike, Jones hurt himself and Ferragamo took over as the number one quarterback of the Los Angeles Rams.

Less Incentive Means Less Leverage

It's nearly always impossible to negotiate a contract with people who are not motivated. My major problem in negotiating with the Rams, or with any NFL team, is that they don't need to win games on the football field in order to make money. The way the new major TV networks' contracts are written, every NFL team starts the season thirteen million dollars in the black! So where is the owner's incentive to pay the ballplayers what they deserve in order to produce a winning team?

Without the possibility of losing money, very few teams are willing—or find it necessary—to pay out large amounts of cash to ballplayers. And don't be misled by the numbers for quarterbacks. When we were negotiating for big money for a quarterback, the average offensive lineman in the NFL was making only $67,000 a year, and how good is a quarterback without an offensive line?

Incentives go both ways. By paying people what they are worth, you are telling them how much you appreciate them. You are telling them you are willing to pay their price because you have faith that they will perform at the top of their form. An employee, by the same token, is motivated by money and appreciation. And money—make no mistake about this—is a *very* powerful form of appreciation!

Taking a Chance

When we are offered opportunities, how many times are we afraid to take a chance? Taking a risk is very much tied in with our aspirations. It's so easy to sit where we are, do nothing, and complain about not doing better in life. But sometimes we are so busy complaining, that we can't see the opportunities coming at us.

I don't mean to suggest you drop everything and go follow a star. But there is no *real* success without taking risks.

Vince could have stayed in Los Angeles and gotten a salary increase, but it would not have been what he deserved—and that was important to him. I didn't know if there was any real chance in Canada. I had to test it. As it turned out, our move started a whole series of events that led to Vince signing a fantastic contract.

It's true that we backed into Canada because of the Rams situation; nevertheless, we were prepared to go up there—and we were lucky to find someone who needed Vince more than Vince needed him. Skalbania would never have thought of Vince if we had not gone up to Canada and talked to Sazio. The principle of risk-taking created the opportunity: The word of Vince's availability went out, and Vince came out a winner.

Time

It's very important to know when you're at an impasse and to stop for a while. When I entered negotiations, I realized there was bad blood between Vince and the Rams. It no longer mattered who was at fault; it was there—and it made for bad negotiations. The only thing to do was to take a break. That's why I told Vince it would be best to break off the talks, play the season, and see what developed.

Sometimes negotiations get too personal. Negotiators are standing out in front; egos and personalities get bruised and the real issues get lost. If negotiations are going nowhere, why continue to butt your head against the wall? The only solution is to pull back, give yourself time. It pays to let the situation brew for a while. Figure out how much time you really can *afford*, and then wait and see what happens.

Plan Ahead

Don't allow your opponent to come to the bargaining table full of facts and figures, ready to bowl you over. If you know a negotiation is coming up, plan for it. Give yourself plenty of time to get all the facts you need to enter into meaningful talks—not only to defend yourself, but to advance your position.

Once I knew I was going to talk to Skalbania, I found out everything I could about the Montreal stadium. I never knew if I would need that information, but it was important to have it at my fingertips. And as you saw, it paid off.

Get It in Writing!

A lot of times people put commitments on a personal level. They'll say, "You can trust me." Well, maybe you can, and maybe if you've done business with them before, you don't need a written commitment. But in most negotiations, you *must* have everything in writing. It not only helps you, but helps the other side. People do a lot of talking in the course of a negotiation; words fly fast and loose. But when words are on paper, they suddenly take on a greater importance. They are binding commitments, things that you can't take back.

With Lou Piniella at Yankee Stadium. *(Credit: Louis Requena)*

Dallas Cowboys wide receiver Drew Pearson, shooting a Xerox commercial.

Vince and me in the locker room of the Hamilton Tiger Cats
of the Canadian Football League.

Dick Schapp, comedian Joe Mauro, Vince Ferragamo, and me at the Royal Canadian Legion dinner in Thunder Bay, Ontario.

The infamous weight-clause
correspondence.

New York Yankees

BILL BERGESCH
VICE-PRESIDENT
BASEBALL OPERATIONS

EXECUTIVE OFFICE
YANKEE STADIUM
BRONX, NEW YORK 10451
(212) 293-4300

March 10, 1982

Messrs. David Fishof

1775 Broadway
New York, New York 10019

Dear David

Per our recent telephone conversations re Lou Piniella and
his excess weight, please be advised of the following stance
the Yankees have adopted.

You are aware of the problem we have in Lou's weight. Despite
his agreement to come to camp at 197 lbs., he came in at 208.
Mr. Steinbrenner spoke with you about Lou and his weight. I
advised you about the fine the Yankees were levying on him.
I wrote Lou advising him that he was being fined the sum of
$1,000.00 per day effective February 22nd.

This year we decided to go to the fine; however, there will be
no such leniency next year. It is in the agreement he will
come in at 200 lbs., it is a definite part of the contract, and we
are most serious about the fact Lou maintains his weight at the
200 lb level so that he can perform to the utmost of his ability.

We hope you will cooperate with us since it is in the best interests of all of us....Lou, you, and the Yankees....that Lou
keep working on his weight program.

Sincerely,

Bill Bergesch
Vice-President
Baseball Operations

New York Yankees

EXECUTIVE OFFICE
YANKEE STADIUM
BRONX, NEW YORK 10451
(212) 293-4300

EDWIN T. BRODERICK
VICE-PRESIDENT-GENERAL COUNSEL

March 9, 1982

Mr. David Fishof
David Fishof Productions
1775 Broadway
New York, New York 10001

Dear Mr. Fishof:

Your letter of February 25, 1982 addressed to Mr. George
Steinbrenner does in no way confirm the agreement between
Mr. Steinbrenner and your client, Lou Piniella.

The agreement is that Mr. Piniella will keep his weight
at under 200 pounds at all times during the season. If
Mr. Piniella's weight is maintained at the 200 pound or less
range during the season, an evaluation will be made as to
whether the fine shall be rescinded. This is the understanding
of the agreement between the New York Yankees and Mr. Piniella.

Thank you very much for your courtesy and cooperation.

Very truly yours,

Edwin T. Broderick
Vice President/
General Counsel

ETB:pl

Mark Estess, Trevor Berbick, and me at a press conference
announcing Trevor's next fight. *(Credit: Miami Herald)*

With Herschel Bernardi backstage at the Mill Run Theater in Chicago.

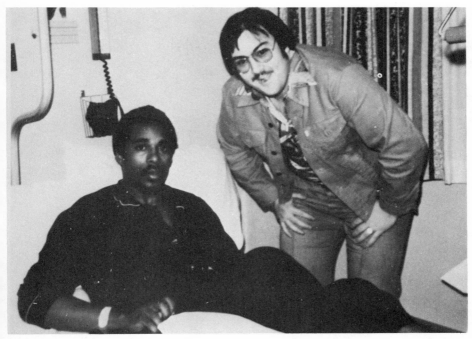

Elliott Maddox recovering from a knee operation in Columbus, Georgia, in 1977.

Mitchell Etess (the entertainment director of Grossinger's) and The Association with the author

Burgess Owens of the Oakland Raiders.

Being interviewed by Bucky Dent on his national cable TV show.

Hacksaw Reynolds demonstrating a variation of his favorite stunt.

With Phil Simms and my daughter Shira at Phil's weekly TV show.

You cannot make a decision until you see the terms completely spelled out. Once you have an offer in writing, look at it not just once, but again and again and again before you make a decision. You've got to be sure of what you're really being offered.

If the people you are negotiating with will *not* put a commitment in writing, you have to be very leery and reconsider your own commitment. You must ask yourself if the offer you are getting is legitimate. Or is it just talk?

Who Makes the Decisions?

One of the biggest frustrations in any negotiation is going through the process, reaching an agreement, and then finding out the person opposite you is not authorized to say yes and unable to make a commitment. That was the problem in the Rams' organization. I was negotiating with General Manager Don Klosterman. Carroll Rosenbloom had died suddenly. Carroll's son, Steve, was out of the picture, and Carroll's wife, Georgia, suddenly found herself the owner of a football team.

Georgia must have been a little concerned; she was the only woman owner in one of the most macho of all sports. I think she was afraid of being overruled by the men who had run the Rams and those who had run the NFL. To protect herself, she told Don Klosterman to go and negotiate, but to come back to her for permission to make any commitment.

Eventually, it became clear that Klosterman was acting as a buffer for the owner. Whatever offer he made had to be acceptable not only to us but to Georgia. He was caught in the middle. He could make us a fair offer, but there was no guarantee Georgia would accept it—and then his face would have egg all over it. As such, there was no way the negotiations could have been conducted in a fair and sincere manner.

The lesson to learn from this is very important in any negotiation. Who are you negotiating with? Ask him what power he has. Can he commit himself to an agreement? Can he sign the agreement? If he can't, find out who has the power and try to get that person into the negotiating process. If your skills or your possessions are *truly* wanted, then the person who can give you what you deserve will come, sit down, and negotiate with you. If not, if the individual sitting opposite you can't give you what you want, there is no sense negotiating—you're wasting your time. Just get up and walk away.

Getting It Now or Later

One of the major stumbling blocks is exactly how much payment is to be made. The NFL's philosophy is pretty much what Klosterman laid out: Put your time in now, and you'll get paid down the line. I don't agree with that as a general principle for *any* occupation, and especially not for football, where a player can get injured today and have *no* future down the line.

Many corporations use the same tactics as the NFL's. Work your way up, they say, and we'll take care of you later. But there are no guarantees: You can be fired tomorrow. The only certainty is your ability *today*. Get paid for what you do *today*. Get the money in your own hands, and take care of your *own* future.

Greasing the Tracks

One of the best tactics (one notable for its absence in the Ferragamo negotiation) is greasing the tracks. It's simple, easy, and relatively inexpensive, and yet few people ever take advantage of it. All it takes is a small show of appreciation of the other person.

When Jack Reynolds went to the Super Bowl in 1982, Bill Walsh gave him a raise without his even asking for it. There, on the table, were a check and a money offer. Obviously appreciation was being shown.

Contrast that with the way the Rams treated Vince. Vince had taken them to the Super Bowl. What would it have cost them to give him a raise in his option year, or even a bonus or a paid vacation? In relation to the money and prestige the Super Bowl had brought the Rams, the outlay would have been minuscule. And, in effect, they would have softened him up for future negotiations. He would have felt *wanted;* he might have felt beholden to them.

Sometimes a small show of appreciation can save, or make, a fortune.

But with Vince, nothing was done. The club's lack of appreciation or any kind of thank-you started the initial negotiations off on a bitter note. Vince was not motivated to give in to their offers the way he might have had he felt they truly appreciated him.

A show of appreciation may not help, but it sure won't hurt. A kind word, a friendly gesture are just some of the ways to get negotiations off to a good start. Not that the other party will give you what you want *merely* because you greased the track, but I do believe that by showing you regard them as people and appreciate them, you move the negotiation away from the bitter, shouting, confrontational aspect and onto a higher plane.

And as a business tool, a show of appreciation is invaluable. I think a good boss should give an employee who's doing well a raise before the employee asks for it. Sometimes people want to see appreciation as much as they want to see dollars.

Test Your Alternatives

One of the reasons I had to consider Canada in Vince's case was because I felt the NFL had me locked into a corner. I had to see if there really was an alternative.

It does no good to sit around and complain. If you are unhappy in your job, you must see what other positions are available. Take a day off, or an evening; apply for a job and see what you're worth. See if there are any other options out there. You may find there are, you may find there aren't—but whatever happens, you'll get a new perspective of what's going on in your field.

You do have to test the water. One of the reasons I went to Canada was to show Vince that he was not necessarily stuck where he was. It was important that he know someone was willing to pay him what he was worth.

Conflict of Interest

As you saw, Paul Caruso kept telling Vince he was handling the negotiations as a favor to Vince. But Caruso was also a friend of Don Klosterman's. This created a potential conflict of interest. Avoid putting yourself in a position like this, or negotiating with someone who has this kind of conflict.

In any deal you have to find out the connections and interests of those people who are negotiating on your behalf and of those who are on the other side of the bargaining table. If there is a conflict, why take a chance that you'll wind up on the short end of the stick?

Premature Commitments

When Paul Caruso negotiated with the Rams, he said he spoke on Vince's behalf. Vince told me that he had given Caruso the right to negotiate for him, but *not* the right to *agree* on a deal.

That is a very important distinction. As you saw, it created a lot of problems: What happened was that Caruso told the Rams they could have Vince for $700,000, plus a retainer fee for himself. The Rams and Caruso shook hands on it, but Vince didn't like the deal. The Rams didn't want to pay any more money. It may not have mattered what Vince was worth. They had made an offer, and Caruso had agreed to it.

The principle involved here is very important. Let's say I have a tape recorder worth $50.00 and I tell you, "I'll sell it to you for ten." You agree, but then I say, "No, I can't sell it to you for ten. You've got to give me thirty-five dollars." Even though you know the tape recorder is worth $50.00, and $35.00 is a bargain, you most likely will not buy it—because I went back on my first offer.

Threats

Threats are a very sharp weapon and must be wielded very, *very* carefully. Terry Bledsoe, assistant general manager of the New York Giants and a negotiator for the NFL Management Council, always quotes George Meany: "The threat of a strike is one thing. The actual strike is another."

You have to understand that. You can *always* threaten. But unless you are absolutely indispensable to the very life of a company, such a threat must always remain only that and *not* an actual fact.

All you've got to do is look at the air-traffic controllers. As long as they were threatening to strike, they had tremendous power. Few people in this country could imagine how the airlines would survive without the air-traffic controllers. Every pilot said they would not fly if the controllers went on strike. The possibility of a disaster seemed incredible. But once the strike actually took place—well, adjustments were made.

That was the same problem with Vince's one-day walkout. Whose interest would it have served? As long as Vince threatened to walk out, he had some negotiating leverage. And by staying in camp, he would be letting his teammates know he was not going to jeopardize their chances of a successful season by being selfish or greedy. It's true the walkout made the *L.A. Times*, but I don't see how that helped Vince Ferragamo. By walking out one day and coming back the next, he proved nothing; in fact, he *lost* leverage in the negotiations.

So, if you negotiate with a threat and suddenly your bluff is called, you have to ask yourself *how* acting on your threat will resolve or force a resolution of the problem.

Third Parties

In negotiations you sometimes have to *act* as if you are not in control of the process. In Vince's case I am sure Klosterman was *not* in control, but his mechanism of saying, "I'll never be able to convince her [Georgia]," was worth leverage and time.

For instance, I can be offered a deal for a client in which I think the offer is too low. It makes no sense to insult the person making the offer, so I say, "I don't think my client will go for it. I'll check with him and get back to you." That way, I have not insulted anybody, and I have kept open the lines of communication.

Ask and Ye Shall Receive

By asking Sazio for two million dollars, what did I have to lose? I felt that if Vince was going to play in Canada, he would have to make enough money to cover not only the football salary he deserved from the Rams, but the loss of endorsement money. By being in Los Angeles, Vince was always in the public eye, doing ads, making personal appearances, endorsing products.

One problem in most negotiations is people are "afraid" to state their demands. They will sit and think about what they want, spelling it out to *themselves*. Most people don't like to get no for an answer; so when it comes down to asking, they rationalize and second-guess their opponents—and come up with a figure they think the other side will accept. Negotiating is a give-and-take situation. Ask for more than what you want, because anyone on the other side of the table is going to *assume* your figures are inflated and they will try to negotiate you down.

What you have to avoid is asking for too much—and here you have to do your homework on your client, on yourself, and on who you are dealing with. In Vince's case I added up his football salary, appearances, and endorsements. Then I had to calculate what a superstar was worth to Canada. With Skalbania, of course, it was more than just throwing the football—Vince was part of Skalbania's overall strategy for establishing himself as a sports kingpin.

It is also important to know when to ask. Sometimes it is much better to listen to the other side before putting all your demands forward.

CHAPTER
5

LESSONS ALONG THE WAY

I t was one of those March days you can sleep through. The calendar on my desk said spring had arrived, but the temperature outside was in the forties and a blustery wind was sweeping down Broadway, sending pieces of old newspapers whirling up into the air. I'd had enough of the cold. Looking out my window at the people scurrying along the street, all bundled up, I kept thinking of going to Florida. Maybe New York would be warm when I got back.

I *could* take off. All I needed was a phone, either to make a deal or to make a plane reservation and be anywhere in a couple of hours.

But I never left New York. Early that afternoon I got a call from Phil Simms, the New York Giants' quarterback. "How've you been, David?"

"Fine, fine. Thinking of Florida . . . maybe getting a little sun."

"Yeah. Sure know what you mean." Phil's a southerner from Lebanon, Kentucky. His voice is as smooth and silky as the bluegrass he claims he was weaned on. Solid at six feet two inches weighing 200 pounds, with blue eyes and blond hair, Phil has an All-American look. So clean-cut, in fact, he once went to Compton Advertising to audition for an Ivory soap commercial.

"Had a great time in Albany," Phil said over the phone.

"Even though you didn't crash?" I kidded. Three weeks before,

Phil had done me a favor. I had booked Drew Pearson, the wide receiver of the Dallas Cowboys, to appear at a Muscular Dystrophy telethon I do every year for station WTEN in Albany. At the last minute I got a call from Pearson's attorney, Ray McCoy. Pearson couldn't be found; he was out hunting, fishing, or something. Anyway, he obviously wasn't going to show up in Albany. I asked Phil to stand in.

He agreed until he heard he had to fly in a small plane. His wife, Diana, is dead set against him flying in small planes, especially in winter, and she was adamant about Albany, where it's windy, cold, and often snowy. But I convinced Phil he'd be okay. It was for a good cause. If he did this favor for me, I'd owe him one.

Now we were chatting until Phil finally worked his way around to the favor he wanted from me. "David, I'm getting a lot of requests for personal appearances. Also a lot of endorsements."

"That's terrific." I waited for the pitch.

"I got a couple agents working on it. I wonder if you'd also be interested."

"How many agents do you have?" I asked.

"Three. I want to see what they come in with, and then I'll go with the best deal." Phil's drawl was laced with satisfaction. He was getting his revenge.

Phil, like a thousand other guys who play college football, had hoped to make it to the NFL. As the quarterback at Moorhead State College, a small school in Kentucky, Phil had had a sensational senior year; and, as sometimes happens with the media, reporters couldn't resist playing up the Cinderella angle.

An agent went down to Moorhead and got Phil's signature on a contract, a one-page letter allowing him to negotiate on Phil's behalf. The surprise came when Phil Simms was the number one draft pick of the New York Giants.

Phil's head was spinning with success. From quarterback at Moorhead (population 2,000) to quarterback at New York (population 10,000,000) is quite a jump. He was young, and not the least bit prepared for the sudden leap to fame. He turned to his agent for advice; he trusted him. The agent took Phil's trust and did a number on him.

Usually an agent gets his commission as the player gets his money throughout the life of the contract. Phil's agent took his full three-years' commission at the signing. Then he got a contract with *Sports Illustrated* for a Phil Simms poster. When the poster was ready for Phil's signature, Phil was out of town. The agent, wanting his money and not wanting to waste any time, signed Phil's name on the poster. Not only did the poster have a forged signature, but the name was misspelled. The agent had signed it Phill instead of Phil.

Then on top of that, Simms—being young and thinking his agent was doing all kinds of things for him—lent the man money out of his own pocket. Now Phil was suing the guy, but it left a very bad taste in his mouth about agents, and he wanted some satisfaction. He thought that by playing a couple of agents against each other, he was going to beat them at their game.

But it was like cutting off his nose to spite his face.

"Phil? You know ————?" I asked him, naming a well-known comic, knowing full well he did.

"Sure. We did a roast together." One of Phil's goals is to get into television sportscasting after his playing days are over. So he does a lot of roasts because he has a good sense of humor. "He's very funny."

"He's also making less money than he should."

There was silence on the other end of the line.

After a few seconds I asked, "You want to know why?"

"Sure."

"Did you ever hear his joke about the William Morris Agency, that they don't get him enough work?"

"Yeah. He tells it all the time."

"He'll be complaining about the Morris agency until he's a hundred and twenty. It's one of his standard jokes." I paused and went on, "Only it's not a joke. The jokes about him having five hundred agents are true. It gets him laughs, but not a lot of leverage. One night he works for five thousand dollars, the next for two thousand."

"Like me."

"You got it." I smiled to myself; it's always nice to know when you're getting through. "Look, Phil, there are only so many deals.

If you have three or four agents representing you on the same deal, you're negotiating against yourself. Each agent will undercut the other to get the job, and *you're the one who's going to lose.*"

"David." The slick accent was gone from Phil's voice. "Will you do me a favor? You be my agent. You handle the deals."

My friend Tony Sciametta is one of the most generous men I know; he's the kind of guy who would rip the shirt off his back for you. He deals in foreign exchange, and millions of dollars are involved every minute. Most of his business is done over the telephone. Oral commitments are made for millions. "It's the nature of the business," Tony explained to me. "Exchange rates are constantly changing. We can't wait for written commitments." The word they use is "done." When they say it's "done," that's it!

I once asked him how he could get people to keep their word.

"Reputation is part of it. But you see," he said, pointing to the phone, "all the calls are on tape. Everyone knows that. So if there is ever a problem, we go back to the client and play the tape."

Tony used to have me book a lot of athletes to make personal appearances for his company. Once he asked me to get Joe DiMaggio to come to a luncheon so his clients could meet the Yankee Clipper. I set it up, but four days before the luncheon, Joe called to tell me he wasn't going to be able to make it.

He had agreed to come because he had planned to be in New York that day to do a television commercial for the Bowery Savings Bank. But the filming was being delayed a week, and he didn't think it was worth coming to New York just for the luncheon. He would come next week.

Tony was in a meeting when I called.

An hour later I got a call. It was Tony. I told him about Joe. "David, why don't you come down here before noon—say forty-five minutes from now. I want to talk to you."

I didn't even look at my appointment calendar to see if I could make it. I knew I had to be there.

Tony had a lesson to teach me. He sat me down and said, "You know, David, I like you. That's why I do business with you. I believe in your word. When you say, 'Done,' I know you mean it."

His eyes bored into me and I felt very uncomfortable. Obviously he was upset about Joe DiMaggio. He had given *his* word that DiMaggio would be at the luncheon; now Joe wasn't going to show. But how could I get the greatest baseball player of all time to change his mind?

He didn't say anything for a few moments, not paying the least attention to my discomfort. Suddenly he leaned forward and I saw fire in his big black eyes. "But I'm not in that business. David, I'll tell you my philosophy. If you have to tell me how much it's going to cost me, I can't afford it. You gave me your word . . . *done*! I expect you to keep it."

Within an hour I found out that Joe DiMaggio was in Las Vegas at the Sands Hotel. I hopped on a plane and was in Vegas by late afternoon. Joe was out on the golf course when I got to the Sands, so I waited. When he came in I walked up to him. "Joe," I said, "you know I have tremendous respect for you. I made a commitment for you for this luncheon. For you, I know it's a small thing. It's not like a TV commercial. But I gave people in New York my word that you would be there."

His friend Harry was with him. Harry turned to Joe and said, "You know, David came all the way here to pick you up and make sure you do this appearance. Joe, I think you should go."

Joe DiMaggio came to New York just for that one afternoon luncheon. Tony was beautiful and treated Joe like the gold he is. Joe was beautiful, too; he understood.

For me—and I think for anyone in business—it's a great lesson. When you make a commitment to someone and say it's "*done*," it's done. I expect the same from anyone I'm dealing with—from my secretaries, from celebrities, from whoever is buying the talent. If it's *not* going to be done, then I want to hear that, too, *and up front*!

I think a lot of people get waylaid in business, and even in their personal lives, by making commitments they never intend to keep. And I don't mean just big things. But more often than not, it's the little things that are remembered. Too often people shrug off the little things, saying, "It doesn't matter." Maybe it doesn't, but the fact that you don't keep your word does. If you keep your word on small items, people will assume you're going to do it on the big ones, too.

Dr. Gil Simon is the pediatrician we and the Piniellas use for our children. One day Monica took our daughter, Shira, in for a checkup, and in the course of the conversation, Dr. Simon mentioned a patient of his, a young boy who was dying, who might last another week or two—maybe a month. The kid's biggest dream was to meet Lou Piniella. Monica asked the doctor to call me. As soon as I heard the story, I called Lou and arranged for seats for that Sunday's game.

The boy was feeling very weak on Friday night and Saturday. "You have to feel better," his mother kept telling him. "You're going to meet Lou Piniella tomorrow."

Before he went to sleep that night he said, "Mommy, I don't want to close my eyes because I'm afraid I won't wake up tomorrow."

"Don't worry, son," she said. "You're going to wake up."

And he did, feeling stronger than he had felt in a long time. He got dressed and he and his parents drove to the ballgame. Lou gave him an autographed ball, and they all posed for pictures together.

That evening, before he went to sleep, the boy looked up at his mother and said, "Mommy, I don't want to live anymore. I met my idol, Lou Piniella."

That night, the boy died in his sleep.

Once I did a marathon booking for Herschel Bernardi. He did Brooklyn College on Saturday night; Philadelphia, Sunday afternoon; New Jersey, Sunday night; Chicago, Monday night; and Detroit, Tuesday night. It wasn't so bad; at $7,500 a performance he made a lot of money for four days' work. He came back to my house in New Jersey, where I was living at the time, and he told my wife and me we were all going to celebrate—Monica, Bernardi, his conductor, Elliott Finkel, and me.

Herschel comes from the old school. When he first started in show business, he had to drive a cab to make a living. He would finish his number but had an arrangement with his piano player to play more notes while he left the stage. Bernardi always kept his cab near the stage door and would get in and drive around to the front of the theater. There, wearing a hat, unrecognized, he would pick people up coming out of the theater and get their reaction to his act. But—the money came hard.

As we were driving around, looking for a place to eat, Herschel spotted a diner in Old Bridge.

"Let's go there," Herschel said. He made me stop the car, and we went in.

I was a little disappointed. After all those bookings, I was looking for a really good restaurant. We sat down and looked at the menu. There wasn't much to choose from. When the waiter came over, Herschel turned to me and said, "Make this guy rich."

That's one of Herschel's lines, that and "Everyone should be rich."

So I looked up at the waiter and said, "What's the most expensive item on the menu?"

"Lobster tails," the waiter replied.

"Good. I'll have an order of lobster tails."

"But David"—Herschel's hand came across the table and touched mine—"you're kosher. You don't eat lobster tails."

"That's right, my friend. I don't eat lobster tails. But I'm ordering the tails, and I'm going to sit here and look at them *and make sure you pay for them.*" It was worth it; we laughed about it for a long time.

Super Bowl XVI was fantastic. I had a fifty-yard-line seat and watched my man, Jack Reynolds, make mincemeat out of the Cincinnati Bengals. After the game I went to the Super Bowl party. Jack Reynolds was sitting outside in the parking lot, tired and cold. He'd been to the party and left. The emotion of playing and winning the Super Bowl was more than enough for one day. All the carrying-on inside was just too much for him, so he was cooling off his overloaded circuits.

I took Jack back to the party. Everyone was happy, drinking, kissing one another. John McVay came over and said, "Thank you, David." He had a great twinkle in his eye.

Jack came by in a little while and nudged me. "Let's go, David. I don't like the food here."

So here we were at one o'clock in the morning, touring Detroit, when Jack spotted a Colonel Sanders Kentucky Fried Chicken joint. We went in. "What do you want, David?"

"Hey, Jack, I can't eat this food. I'm kosher."

"Oh, yeah, I forgot." Jack turned to the guy at the counter and said, "It's only for me. Give me the big bucket over there."

"Ten pieces, man?" the clerk asked.

"Yeah. That's fine."

We took the chicken, went out, and sat in the car. Jack said nothing; he just sat there eating one piece of chicken after another as I watched in amazement. Hours before, seventy million people had watched Jack make the greatest defensive plays in Super Bowl history. Now he was sitting in a parking lot eating fried chicken.

We sat up all night talking about the game, but there were long spells of quiet when Jack must have been reflecting on the victory. Jack had done most of his "communicating" that afternoon, and I was just happy to be with him, to share his moments of glory.

Defensive lineman Gary Jeter was in his option year with the New York Giants when I went to them to discuss a new contract. He was restless so I asked for a trade, possibly to a team in Florida since Gary has friends on both the Dolphins and the Buccaneers. The Los Angeles Rams showed interest, however, and a trade was made. After all, he was an alumnus of USC and could once again be reunited with coach John Robinson and defensive line coach Marvin Goux. I was excited.

I called John Shaw at the Rams office in Beverly Hills for an appointment to discuss Gary's contract, and I flew to Los Angeles to meet with him.

As it turned out, John wouldn't even consider negotiating a contract with Gary because he was in an option year and had injured himself last season. "Too risky," were John's final words. I couldn't understand this sudden turnabout in his feelings.

Our meeting had ended and it was Friday afternoon in Los Angeles. I suggested to John that we go out and spend the rest of the day together. He agreed and our first stop was at William Morris to visit my friend Tom Illius. Tom is known for representing and booking major stars in Las Vegas, Lake Tahoe, and Reno.

We walked into his office and I introduced John. "Tom," I said, "John won't give me a contract for Jeter. He's questioning his knee injury."

Tom turned to John and said, "You know, I book shows at casinos fifty-two weeks a year. Some shows are winners and some aren't. If I could predict and book only those shows that would be a success, I would be in business for myself. In other words, some things you hit on and some you don't. Since you can't predict winners all the time, why don't you at least give your business to David?"

Although John responded with a laugh, I knew the idea was implanted in his mind.

Two weeks later, John called me and was willing to negotiate Gary's contract.

One day I got a call from Dennis Arfa, Billy Joel's agent, who told me Billy Joel would love to meet Lou Piniella. Would Lou and his wife and I like to come over for dinner?

I called Lou. "Lou, Billy Joel wants you over for dinner."

"Great, David," Lou said. "Fifteen hundred."

You must remember that Lou makes a lot of personal appearances, dinners for benefits, and part of his income is from those appearances. "Lou." I laughed. "It's not a personal appearance. It's Billy Joel, the singer. It's a dinner party for you."

"Okay, make it a thousand."

Now I was roaring. "It's Billy Joel, the singer." I repeated.

I heard Lou ask Anita, "You ever heard of Billy Joel?"

"Ever heard of him?" Anita shouted. "I love him. What about him?"

"David wants us to go to dinner with him. David, Monica, you, and me to dinner at Billy Joel's house."

"Are you kidding?" Anita rushed up to the phone. "Let's go!"

Bobby Murcer and his wife, Kay, were sitting in the Piniella's living room. I heard Bobby shout, "Hey, I want to go, too, for a free album." We made an arrangement for us all to go and have dinner at Billy Joel's house after a ball game.

The wives wanted to take pictures. Anita had called Monica to tell her to be sure to bring an Instamatic. I told Monica not to take a camera. It seemed an intrusion. Lou and Bobby told their wives not to take cameras. The women protested, but Lou put his foot down—*no cameras!*

So we went out to Long Island without cameras. The wives were bawling; they wanted a souvenir—and they got it! The minute we walked into the house, Billy Joel was there with an Instamatic taking pictures of all of us.

Big, strong, tough Jack Reynolds was drinking milk, doing it for the California Dairy Association. The association was using different celebrities—Valerie Perrine, Jimmy Walker. Jack was their sports personality.

Jack was shown in a T-shirt, looking rugged, with one foot on a Jeep. A series of lines was used: "I'm a tough guy, but even tough guys like me drink milk." "Milk is good for you." "It's delicious to drink." At the end of the commercial, Jack, who is holding a glass of milk, has to drink it.

Jack likes milk; he does drink it, but today it wasn't relaxing him. We'd been at it for hours, starting at eight in the morning, and it was now three in the afternoon. All for a thirty-second spot! It was reminiscent of a show business motto: "Hurry up and wait." We were up to the fiftieth take, and everyone was trying to figure out how to get Jack to loosen up so we could finish the commercial.

I'd been watching Jack and knew that between takes he'd been drinking beer.

"Take away the beer," I said. "Put it in the milk carton and keep it in front of him. That way he knows he can't get the beer until he finishes the lines in the commercial."

Sure enough, with the milk carton filled with beer in front of him, Jack breezed through the next four takes and we had a print.

One day, just before a game, Lou Piniella was sitting in the dugout and was hungry. He called the bat boy over and gave him some money to get some cheeseburgers across the street at McDonald's.

The kid brought back the cheeseburgers, but Lou got only one bite before the Yankees had to take the field. It's against the rules to eat on the field, but Lou was still hungry. So he put a cheeseburger into the pocket of his glove, covered it with his hand, and ran out into right field.

He knew the fans were watching him and the TV cameras were panning the stadium. He brought his glove up to his face as if spitting into the pocket, but actually he was taking little nips from his cheeseburger.

In the meantime all the other Yankees were throwing the ball around, warming up. The ball kept going between Reggie Jackson and Mickey Rivers, but no one threw it to Lou Piniella. Nobody knew what was going on.

The game started. The first pitch was a fly to—you guessed it—Lou Piniella. He glided over and snagged it. The ball fell right into the center of his glove. Without missing a beat, Lou took the ball out and ripped it to Willie Randolph at second.

If you look at the replay, you can see Randolph's disgusted expression as he scoops the greasy ball out of his glove.

I was in Reno, dining with Fred Travalena, who I booked. He was opening the show at Harrah's for Joan Rivers. When I looked at Joan, I was reminded of the story Lisa Jacobson once told me. Lisa and her husband, Leonard, had a small theatrical agency where Joan worked as a secretary when she was trying to make it in show business. Joan had an address book in which she wrote down the name of everyone she met—people who would, she hoped, help her along in her career. Joan vowed if she wasn't a star by the time she filled the book, she would quit the business. Joan met thousands of people and was always writing in her book. And true to her vow, she made it before she filled her book. A little stratagem helped: When she got down to the last two spaces, she started writing in pencil.

Joan was sitting at the table next to us, and we got into a conversation about Jack Segal, an agent in New York, now a man nearing eighty. He'd been around a long time. Jack was a special kind of agent. He pushed unknown talent. He cajoled and talked owners into using his people. He made very little money with them, and then the ones that began heading for stardom left Jack and went on to other agents. He handled some big names—Buddy Hackett and Jackie Mason—but they all left him before he could make money on them. Now he was flat broke.

Jack used to be Joan's agent, pushing her for $50.00 a night when no one wanted Joan Rivers. She never forgot. As we were talking, Joan opened her purse, took out her checkbook, wrote a check, ripped it out, and said, "David, give Jack this money." As she held the check out to me, I could see it was for $5,000.

She was holding one end of the check, I was holding the other end, but she didn't let go. "Don't give him the *check*," she said. "Cash it. Just give him the five thousand dollars. He gave me my first start in show business." Her face was serious, very reflective—she was one of the lucky ones. "I want to help, but don't tell him where the money came from. Just say, 'Here, it's a gift from someone nice.'"

There is a Talmudic saying that the best way to give charity is to give it anonymously. Not only does it leave the receiver free of obligation, it ensures the giver will reap an equal reward, if not an even greater one. I don't know if Joan is a Talmudic scholar, but what she did was certainly from the bottom of her heart.

One of the reasons players hire agents is that when they go in themselves to negotiate, owners generally try to downgrade a player's skill and contribution. An owner will always say how awful a player is, how he's not living up to his potential, all in the hopes of paying him as little as possible.

One owner is different: Al Davis of the Raiders. Burgess Owens is a free safety. The Jets traded him to the Raiders the year they won the Super Bowl, and Burgess thought it was the perfect time to renegotiate the terms of his contract. Although not a client of mine, Burgess is one of my best friends, and he asked my advice. "Go see Al," I suggested. "He has a great reputation. He'll give you a fair hearing."

When Burgess walked in to talk to Al, he expected the same kind of treatment he got from the Jets, who had talked down his ability and therefore his worth to the team. But he was in for a surprise.

"How can I help you?" Al asked.

"I want to talk about my contract. I deserve more money."

"Burgess," Al said, his voice confidential, friendly, not the least bit confrontational. "I want to tell you something. You're a hell of a player. You know"—Al sat back in his chair and smiled at Burgess—"we scouted you while you were in high school. Remember your senior year? Those four interceptions you made in that one game?" Before Burgess came in, Al had told his staff to do a complete bio on Burgess, so he knew everything about the man.

Burgess was speechless. You must remember, he believed he had been traded because he was the team player representative, and a very vocal one at that. Most NFL owners have a fondness for trading player reps.

"And Florida State!" Al got up and started walking around his desk. "We were watching you. We always wanted you, but the Jets beat us. They wouldn't let us have you." Al was now sitting on the edge of his desk, his face inches away from Burgess's. "You're an asset, and we're proud to have you here."

What could Burgess say? He felt terrific. In less than a minute, Al Davis had made him feel more wanted and appreciated than he'd felt in all the years he played with New York.

"You don't even have to tell me what you want," Al said as he walked back around the desk and sat down. "I'm going to give you an extra ten thousand dollars because I know you're going to be a great help to us and the Raiders are damn glad to have you as part of our organization."

Now what could Burgess do? He said, "Thank you," got up, and walked away. How could he ask for more money from a man like that?

Al Davis is smart. Money is important, but he knows all people have to feel important. And that's what he does—he makes you feel important and saves himself a lot of hassle and money.

The contract I negotiated for Lou Piniella with George Steinbrenner called for Lou to come into 1982 training camp at 200 pounds. Lou came into camp overweight.

Most of the other athletes I represent are health conscious, but Lou likes his beer and his cigarettes. Still, he produces; he gets his home runs and timely hits because he's a winning ballplayer—no matter what kind of shape he's in.

It isn't shape that gets hits; it's eye and stroke. And for shape, look at Babe Ruth, the greatest hitter of all time. His paunch always got home before him, but what counted was the art of hitting and his ability to *get* home. Lou Piniella is like that. In 1982 he once again led the Yankees in hits with men on base.

Anyway, the contract I negotiated called for Lou to be at 200 pounds one week before spring training. He came into camp the last week of February at 207 pounds. Perfect for George Steinbrenner—he had a story for the media. George didn't talk to Lou about the weight; instead, he complained to the press and to the TV sportscasters. And because Lou is popular in New York, and all the baseball writers and sportscasters were in Fort Lauderdale, the story got headlines.

George called me. "David, we made a deal." He was screaming at me. I could hardly understand him. "You and I agreed Lou would come in at two hundred pounds."

Then Lou was on the phone to me. "David, you gotta come down here or I'm walking away. The publicity is crazy. Everyone's hounding me, and I can't get in shape."

I knew Lou's weight wasn't the real problem. Now that Reggie Jackson was gone, George was looking for someone to beat up on.

I spoke to George again. "George," I asked, "why are you making such a to-do? Lou came into camp a week early just so he could lose the extra weight. Give him till March first."

"Yeah," George bellowed at me. "March first and from then on, he's going to be fined one thousand dollars a day for every day he's overweight."

"That's a pretty stiff fine, George."

"Well, that's what it is."

I was sure the fine would be the big news item that night. If George was telling *me*, he'd already told the media, and when Lou heard it, he'd blow up. I had to talk to Lou before the reporters got to him.

Too late! By the time I got Lou on the phone, he knew all about the fine, and he was steaming. I called Marvin Miller, head of the Major League Baseball Players Association, and complained that the fine was excessive. Marvin asked me if I wanted to make a formal complaint and go into arbitration.

I knew Steinbrenner hates arbitration. He thinks it's a personal insult. No need to add any more fuel at this point! "No, Marvin, not yet. Let's see what I can work out."

The hassling went on for weeks. With the Yankees playing

lousy ball, the only story coming out of Florida was the feuding between George Steinbrenner and Lou Piniella.

Finally I called Bill Bergesch, the Yankee vice-president, and George's right-hand man. "Bill, we have to get this weight business straightened out."

"Sure thing, David. Can you come down tomorrow and meet George? We're in Palm Beach against the Expos."

First thing in the morning I caught a plane to Palm Beach. There was a ticket waiting for me at the ball park, and my seat was right behind George, Cedric Tallis, and Bill Bergesch. George knew I was there the minute I sat down, but he didn't turn around right away to say hello—playing it cool. After a few innings, he finally did turn around and gave me a big greeting, all very cordial.

I sent a note through an usher to tell Lou that I was there. When Lou got the note, he walked out of the dugout, left the playing area through a small gate, and met me behind the stands. In Fort Lauderdale there are open stands like sandlot ball parks throughout the country. Lou's coming off the playing field was against the rules. He did it because he knew Steinbrenner was watching him. "David, get me out of here. I don't care what it takes. I've had it."

"Lou, take it easy. George and I are going to talk. Lou . . . he's complaining about the weight."

"I'm in good shape." Lou was defensive. "I'm hitting the ball. That's what counts, that's what he's paying me for. I'm losing the weight."

"Let me handle it," I told Lou. "If George doesn't want you on the team, he'll fine you, then suspend you. *Then* we'll make a deal."

While we were talking, the fans came over to Lou and asked for his autograph. He was signing it automatically, without even looking or stopping our conversation. I told Lou, "Don't worry, I'll straighten it all out."

Sitting behind George Steinbrenner at a Yankee game is an experience. George fights every call against the Yankees, turning everything—a ball, a strike, an out, a hit—into a contest between him and everyone else. Watching Steinbrenner carrying on, I suddenly felt very sympathetic toward the players in the club. It must be very tough having George sit there, watching and *judging* every move. And mind you, this was spring training, when they were rusty and just beginning to get into shape.

A lot of players have told me how awful it is when a guy grounds out when George is sitting behind the first-base line. "You give it your all, but you're out. You can't be safe all the time. But then you turn around and see George's reaction—contempt and anger as if it's a personal affront to him—it makes you feel bad."

I made arrangements with Bergesch to talk to George after the game. I approached him as he was walking toward his car. "George, we have to talk."

Steinbrenner looked at me. "Talk to Cedric or Bill."

"George, I came down here to talk to you." I was becoming angry at getting a runaround. "You were the one who said, 'I made a deal with you.' Well, so we have to talk. I came down here to talk to you, not them."

George brushed me aside. "No! Talk to them. I don't have the time. I'm busy; I have to catch a plane." And with that he got into his car, and the chauffeur closed the door.

Cedric Tallis, who was standing there, said, "Come on, David. I'll give you a lift."

I got into Tallis's car, and suddenly I remembered I had left my suitcase in the Expos' office.

"Cedric, wait a minute," I said, getting out of the car. "I just have to get my bag. I'll be right back."

I got my bag and was back in less than five minutes, but all the cars were gone. No one was there! When George took off, everyone had to follow him back to his office in Fort Lauderdale.

I was steaming. I went into the Yankee dressing room and saw Lou, who offered to take me to Fort Lauderdale on the team bus.

Instead, I went with Al Mary. Al is an old friend who wrote for the *Westchester Gazette*, and he comes down to spring training every year. By the time we got to Fort Lauderdale, George had changed his plans and could meet me. George, Cedric, and Bill were all waiting for me. At first, I was a little upset at this arrangement. George was there with his team; I was alone. It was three against one, but Bill and Cedric are first-rate gentlemen and I knew I had to settle this with George, so it really didn't matter who was there. I was going to act as if the two of us were alone.

"David," George started, "it specifically states in the contract that Lou has to come in at two hundred pounds. He's overweight; it's a bad image for the Yankees."

I was listening to this from George Steinbrenner, who's anything but a streamlined specimen. He was the one creating the "Yankee image."

"Lou came into camp early to work out so he could lose weight."

"Well, he didn't."

"He did. On March first, he weighed two hundred pounds."

"He's overweight. It looks bad!" George shouted at me.

"George"—my voice was placating—"you know what happened. After all that publicity about his weight, Lou got to two hundred pounds on March first and was very happy with himself. After all"—I paused and smiled at George—"he did what *you* asked him. A lot of the other players were proud of him, and they went out that night and celebrated. He ate too much and gained back a few extra pounds."

"Yeah," George frowned. "A few extra pounds that he still has. The contract stipulated two hundred pounds."

Steinbrenner was watching me like a cat ready to leap on a mouse, but I was sure *I* was the cat. "He's *not* in violation of the terms of the contract," I said quietly but forcefully.

"He is! He's overweight."

"No, George. If you read the contract properly, it says that Lou must report on March first at two hundred pounds. Lou weighed two hundred pounds on March first!" I looked at George. "There's nothing in the contract that says he has to *maintain* a weight of two hundred pounds."

Within ten minutes we got rid of the fine—$7,000—and agreed that Lou would maintain his weight at 203 pounds. Everyone was happy; I saved Lou some money, and George had several more weeks with the Yankees and his name in the headlines.

CHAPTER
6

SELLING YOURSELF

I didn't get into this business because I set out to be an agent, but because opportunities were presented to me and I worked at them.

But I'm lucky even to have had the opportunities presented. In a sense, I'm lucky to be alive. My father, Mark Fishof, lived in Nitra, near Bratislava, Czechoslovakia. In March 1942 the Gestapo arrested him and sent him to a labor camp in Eastern Europe. My father escaped and made his way to Hungary. He spoke German and was an experienced stamp maker. For eighteen months he lived in Budapest as a non-Jew, working in an engraving shop. The Nazis used the shop for making identity papers, and my father used to "borrow" special stamps, duplicate them, and then use them to forge papers. There are hundreds of people in America whose forged identity papers, thanks to my father, enabled them to flee Hungary. But near the end of 1943, he got caught and was shipped to Auschwitz and then to Buchenwald.

My father survived. He came to America after the war and went into business with his brother in a rubber-stamp and printing shop in Brooklyn, and married my mother, Edith.

My brother, Joey, was born in New York City in 1950, and I was born in June 1956. When I was two years old, my father had had enough of the printing business and accepted a job as a cantor in Galveston, Texas.

Even as a kid, I was full of energy, always on the go, constantly moving around. I loved the excitement of meeting people, talking to them, selling them things. When I was six, I wrote and printed a newspaper in my apartment and sold copies to all the people living in the building. My uncle had bought a ton of pens and pencils at an auction, and I unloaded them all at school.

From my father I learned to relate to people. Many clergymen think they're smarter than the people who come to their synagogues and churches. Not only that, they believe they're closer to G-d. But all they have is a little more education and religion. My father always said that whoever came into the synagogue was his boss; they were paying his salary. Not only did he have to have a good voice, he had to be liked. His personality was as important as his singing. He understood he had to have presence. He always dressed well, looked neat and clean, and always had a kind word for everyone. It was interesting that in my childhood years the men who used to criticize my father were the ones who had bosses over them. But those men who had businesses of their own always had the utmost respect.

We stayed in Galveston until 1961. Then on to Brockton, Massachusetts, known for its shoes and Rocky Marciano, where my father became a cantor in Congregation Agudas Achim. My mother was a college student at Bridgewater State Teachers College. In 1966 my father took a position at Temple Beth El in Hackensack, New Jersey. (From Galveston to Brockton to Hackensack—you can see I come from hick towns.)

We always seemed to live in neighborhoods where most of the kids weren't Jewish. I was dealing with older men in their forties, fifties, and sixties; men who were members of my father's synagogue and came to *shul;* men and women who were friends of my parents and came by the house. My parents taught me how to care about other people; that's how you get along.

Sports wasn't one of the subjects that came up in our house, except for Spanish soccer, which my father always watches, with the sound off. Nor was there any discussion of show business, for that matter. But from a very early age I was turned on by the give-and-take between people. My uncle, Latislav, used to print wedding invitations and, on occasion, he would make a mistake in the date or the time. But he wouldn't throw the misprints away. Instead, he would make a deal—he would sell the customers the

invitations at a discount and convince them to change the date of
the wedding to match the already printed invitations!

Right after the move to New Jersey, my brother, Joey, learned
to play the drums—by ear. He can't read music and never took a
lesson, but the more he played the better he got. I naturally
looked up to my brother, and I wanted to be a musician and play
the guitar. At that time, I had no idea why. Years later, I realized
my motives weren't to be a musician, but simply to be like him.

To make matters worse, my father wanted Joey to have a Jewish education, and sent him to Yeshiva High School in Long
Beach, New York, where Joey became a member of the band. For
years all I wanted was to become a musician in my brother's band.
I was taking music lessons, but my father tried to discourage me
from going into the same profession as my brother because he
perceived the envy that was in me. Coming from a family of
twelve brothers and sisters, my father could easily predict the
conflict coming up. I was so frustrated, I didn't know what to do
with my feelings. At fifteen and sixteen, I was in full rebellion,
opposing my parents at every turn.

My father noted the growing tension, and finally one day, he
took me aside. We sat in the study, his private place in the house,
its walls lined with Talmudic books. I was sitting on the edge of
my chair, waiting, expecting him to allow me to work with my
brother's band. Unbeknownst to me, my show business career
was about to begin.

"David . . ." His eyes were so kind, so full of concern. "Instead
of being the performer in the band, be the guy backstage taking
the money."

He knew me. He had seen me always running around buying,
selling, trading, wheeling and dealing. His words cut through all
the pressure in my head. Seeing he'd gotten through to me, he
went on: "Instead of trying to join the band, go out and book it. If
you *play*, you can only be in one place at a time. But if you *book*
bands, you can book ten bands for the same night—in ten different places."

My father, the Spinoza of Hackensack, had spoken, and I could
feel the world beginning to open up in front of me. I am sure the
survival instinct, so strong in him, was passed on to me. What-

ever drove him to survive became mixed in the free soil and air of America and pushed me to success. He had survived the horror; I would make him proud of surviving.

Naturally I was thinking of one thing only—booking my brother's band. This was a Jewish rock-and-roll group called the Ruach Revival. It toured the States playing for Jewish youth organizations, mostly in local synagogues. I would show my brother; I was going to book him into Grossinger's—big stuff! Grossinger's is the top entertainment spot in the Catskills, and for a band like my brother's, Grossinger's was the big time.

The entertainment director at Grossinger's for over thirty years was Jerry Weiss. In all the years that Jerry has controlled entertainment at Grossinger's, he very rarely books acts he hasn't heard. I called him. Never having heard of me, nor of my brother's band, the Ruach Revival, he was polite to me, but not interested in the band. When I called him the following week, he was still polite. "They're not quite right for Grossinger's."

Of course, I had to learn that being an agent is a lot more than picking up a phone. And I learned it from some old pros at the game.

When I was seventeen and had just finished high school, I met Aaron Toder, whose company was called Variety Artists. Toder and his former partner, Hy Einhorn, were known to have pulled one of the great coups in the Catskills, booking the Supremes into Grossinger's. At that time, in July 1971, the Supremes were at the top of the charts and commanded big numbers, more than Grossinger's would pay. But Toder and Einhorn wanted the prestige of having booked them, so they agreed to the Grossinger offer and told the Supremes they would give them their price.

The difference was a couple of thousand bucks. Toder and Einhorn had to find that money; and being the kind of men they were, they certainly weren't going to pull it out of their own pockets.

They called the Monticello racetrack and sold the Supremes for a Sunday midafternoon personal appearance, just signing autographs. Toder and Einhorn were going to cover the difference *and* make some money. Only when they went to collect the Supremes Sunday morning, the three women didn't want to get out of bed. They were too tired, having worked late Saturday night.

Toder and Einhorn didn't panic for even a second. Quickly they found three black chambermaids in Grossinger's, fitted them into the Supremes' dresses and wigs, and put them into the rented limo. That Sunday afternoon all three girls spent two and a half hours signing autographs at the Monticello track.

Toder, a concentration camp survivor, had a thick European accent and dressed very dapperly. He believed that because he was living on borrowed time, he could do whatever he wanted. Consequently, he was fearless.

His office was like a stage setting for a 1950's comedy about show business. The walls were covered with photos; shots of Toder with famous stars from all over the world, and signatures scrawled on them with dedications to him. All very impressive. Not so the rest of the office—a rolltop oak desk and a battered chair, a piano for singers to audition, and a couch.

Aron Toder was an operator, and I suppose I should have known better when I made my salary deal with him to draw $100 a week against commissions. After the season we were going to split whatever profits he made on the acts I booked that summer.

Sure! Being a naïve yeshiva boy who didn't know what was going on, I spent my first summer touring the Catskills and visiting every bungalow and small hotel that featured live entertainment, convincing the owners to use whatever acts Toder was representing. I had never heard of most of them, but neither had the owners. So I used Henny Youngman's material to sell them. And I sold most of the acts, at $100, $150 a night.

In September I innocently showed up at his office ready to collect. He told me there were no profits. Like a brassy kid, I threatened to sue and ran to his lawyer.

Leonard Schindler was a big burly man in a rumpled suit, always with a big cigar in his mouth.

"Kid," he said to me in his gravelly voice, "how much does it cost to go to college?"

"College?" I asked, steaming. "I don't know."

"Take a guess." He relit his cigar and blew smoke all over the place. I couldn't even see his face, fat as it was.

"Ten thousand dollars?" I answered.

"That's what you just got, kid. A ten-thousand-dollar education."

Having gotten my "education," I decided to open up my own office. What the hell! I was so excited. I rented space at 1650 Broadway. Seventeen, with my own business. My name was on the door, I had a red telephone, and I was ready to roll. But I needed stationery.

Morris Drucker was a printer in New York City. I had met him and his family one Passover when I was a maître d' at the Grand Mountain Hotel in Greenfield Park, New York. He and his family became my friends. Now I went to see him and told him what I needed.

He showed me paper samples and styles of type. He suggested what would look best and told me what it would cost. I was really feeling terrific, a big shot.

By this time I had started Bernard Baruch College in New York City, but it was hard going to school and running my office late every afternoon and all weekend. One day I met Arnold Graham (Graham as in Goldberg) in the elevator of 1650 Broadway. Graham was vice-president of the Charles Rapp Agency, the largest agency in the Catskills and my biggest competition.

Graham told me I was making an impact in the mountains, taking business away from him, and suggested I stop by his office for a little chat.

When I did, he offered me a job. I could continue going to college and work out of his office. The agency would pick up all the expenses on the acts I booked, and we would split the commissions, fifty-fifty. Rapp was no Toder, and I took the deal.

I knew exactly where my first call would be. Now with Rapp behind me, I had some clout. I called Jerry Weiss, who eventually was to become my confidant, best friend, and greatest supporter. Now he agreed to book my brother's band into Grossinger's, at $350 for one night.

It had taken me a year and a half to make the deal, but finally I had gotten what I was after. The money wasn't that much: The commission to the agency was only $35.00, my personal share, $17.50. It was the sense of achievement that mattered. The booking was a concrete example of what I could achieve when I went after a goal.

One night several years later, I was at Carnegie Hall emceeing a concert for an organization called the Student Struggle for Soviet Jewry. The headliner was Rodney "I Don't Get No Respect" Dangerfield. (That night I paid him $2,500; now a single night gets him $50,000 and more.) My brother's band was also on the program; and my mother was walking around backstage proudly, smiling, telling everyone she saw, "Look, look, my two sons—on the stage of Carnegie Hall."

But I'm getting ahead of myself. For the next two years, I visited every bungalow community and hotel in the Catskills, booking mostly comedians—Van Harris, Morty Gunty, Mal Z. Lawrance, Joe Mauro, and even a Korean, Johnny Yune, who told Jewish jokes and sang Israeli tunes.

Almost all were one-night engagements. I was always hassling for an extra twenty or fifty bucks; and then after the show, the owner inevitably said he was deducting $25.00 from the fee because the performer's act wasn't long enough. That's chiseling, but what can you do?

Many people who continually work the Catskills have no higher ambitions in show business. They find it easier to drive from Brown's Hotel to Grossinger's than to get on a plane; they're not interested in playing Cleveland, Chicago, Atlanta, or Dallas. They don't want to move around America and try to build a following, get some publicity and exposure. Content to work for guaranteed money and make a decent living, they *know* they can work the Catskills, so why take a chance?

Most people get caught up in the way they are living and continue doing the same thing over and over again. In fact, it was happening to me. I was in the same rut as my clients. Rapp had made money on the people I was representing, they were content and expected to continue making money in the Catskills, no matter *who* made it for them.

Never once in two years did the agency show any appreciation for what I was doing. Sure, I was earning my fair share, but there is more to life than money. Any successful relationship between an employer and an employee has to involve a show of appreciation.

(The Rams must have believed Reynolds was washed up at thirty-four, and therefore they released him. But San Francisco needed his experience. He brought his talent and skill with him; that was in the contract, but it was the 49ers' appreciation that got his heart and made him go the extra mile. Jack went out and played his tail off. That extra mile was a major factor that contributed to Coach Bill Walsh's success in leading the 49ers to the Super Bowl victory in 1982.)

So here I was going around in circles in the Catskills, working for someone who didn't give a damn about me. I was making a decent living, but I aspired to a higher level of excitement and success—only I didn't know where to find it. (You must remember, I was still only nineteen.) Then an opportunity came knocking.

In 1975 I was spending weekends at Camp Togola at Sackett Lake in the Catskills. One afternoon Julius Erving came to the camp to shoot baskets, play with the kids, and sign autographs. Dr. J. put on a spectacular show as usual. He was a walking hurricane, with energy and commotion all around him. Five hundred people were clapping in steady rhythm as he put on an unbelievable dunking exhibition. Everyone in camp—kids, adults—all wanted to get near him, talk to him, touch him. It's a truism that people want to be near the successful. Who knows? Maybe they think some of it will rub off on them. But I was feeling the excitement, and I, too, wanted to be part of it.

While I was watching Dr. J. sign autographs, the owner came by. "It's crazy, huh?" he said. "How excited everyone is."

"It sure is," I replied.

I could feel something happening inside me, something working in my head. It hadn't taken any shape yet, but it was beginning to form. "How much do you pay him?" I asked.

"Twenty-five hundred dollars."

"For two hours' work?" I stared at Dr. J. Twenty-five hundred!

"It's worth it, David," said the owner, patting my shoulder. "These kids are going to remember they met Julius Erving at Camp Togola. They'll come back year after year and send their kids—when they have them."

I couldn't believe it. I was struggling to sell comedians at $150 to $250. I was constantly afraid they would get lost on the mountain roads, or, worse, not be funny. And here was Julius Erving, making $2,500, and all he had to do was show up to do his thing. He is always accepted even before he arrives, even before he does anything. He doesn't have to sing or dance, or make people laugh or cry; for instant recognition and acceptance, all he has to do is be Julius Erving.

The idea was taking definite form inside my head. I knew what I was going to do, and I saw the next turn of my career stretching out in front of me. The owner knew I was an agent. I turned to him. "Would you like to have another athlete up here?"

"Sure," he said. "I'm interested in a baseball player. A Yankee. Do you have any?"

"Give me forty-eight hours, and you'll have one."

"But David, I only want to spend four or five hundred dollars. It doesn't have to be a big name."

Big name, small name. I didn't know any athletes. I was an avid Boston Red Sox fan, and at that time I probably couldn't even have named ten baseball players on the New York Yankees. But that wasn't going to stop me from getting a Yankee for an appearance.

In those days I was writing a weekly entertainment column for *The Jewish Press*, a local New York newspaper. From then on, my readers were going to have to put up with my adding sports stories to the column; I was out to develop a new career. I called Marty Appel, publicity director of the Yankees. "Marty," I said, "I'm doing a big feature on Jewish ballplayers for the press. I want to use Ron Bloomberg." Bloomberg was the Yankees' first baseman. "I need a press pass to come in and talk to Ron. Can we do it tomorrow?"

"It'll be at the gate," Marty said, and I was on my way.

Ron wasn't interested in going to Camp Togola, but he introduced me to Elliot Maddox for a story for *The Jewish Press*.

Maddox, the Yankee centerfielder, is black and was thinking of converting to Judaism. It would make a terrific story. But more important for the moment, since Maddox was on the injured list, he was interested in going to Camp Togola. We agreed on a $400 fee, less my 10 percent commission.

Thirty hours after I had agreed to bring the camp owner a baseball player, I called him, very excited. This was my first sports deal, and double what I normally booked. But the owner had changed his mind. Suddenly it was too late in the season, and he was not interested.

I was stuck. I had promised Maddox an appearance for $400. He was counting on it, and if I wanted to get into this business, I had to come through. I didn't want any word to get out that I was just a talker who can't deliver.

I got hold of the *Yellow Pages* and started going through the list of camps. The thirty-first camp owner I called—Irv Bader of Seneca Lake—said yes. But Bader was willing to spend only $300, and I agreed to it. I'd make up the difference; I had to keep my word to my client. In my business my only asset is my reputation.

But my calls to the other thirty camps weren't wasted. I had been careful to write down the names of the people I spoke with, and the following year I booked athletes into fifteen of them. But now, Maddox and I drove up to Seneca Lake. For me it was an incredible day. A professional athlete—big, tall, a great physical specimen, literally and figuratively someone to look up to—is like a flower drawing bees. An athlete's accomplishments are always with him, like degrees attached to a name. And most important is the idea of aspiration. An athlete is someone who has made it to a position of success and fame that most people in our society aspire to. And most important, many athletes come from humble beginnings, just like the rest of us. If they can make it, we can.

I was on a roll, and my instincts kept me going. On the way back to New York, I asked Maddox, "How would you like to go into business with me, representing athletes?"

Maddox looked at me.

"You make the contacts. I'll book them, and we'll split the commission fifty-fifty."

Here I was, a nineteen-year-old kid, inviting the Yankees' centerfielder to join me in a business, asking a superstar to be my partner. But Maddox agreed!

He introduced me to his friends in the media. Dick Schaap, for one, gave us some play in *Sport Magazine*. We were on our way.

Again, with a minimum of money, I opened an office. My name was back on the door, and I had another red telephone.

The partnership with Maddox lasted only a few months. He got traded to the Baltimore Orioles and then became a free agent. When he got his million-dollar contract with the Mets, he was settled for life and saw no reason to stay in business.

Okay with me. I was back on my own again, but this time I knew exactly where I was heading. My name was never going to come off the door again.

7

WINNING WITH KINDNESS

Y ou've seen me in action. You've sat at my elbow as I've negotiated, and you've seen how the results were achieved. You've also seen the whys behind the headlines—the personal and business motivations and machinations that made all the participants act the way they did.

You've seen some of the techniques I've used, and as you read on, you'll see many more that you can use in *your* everyday life. But once you get what you deserve, you don't want to be left with a bitter taste in your mouth or a guilty feeling for the way you acted. Behind these techniques for achieving success, there must be some philosophy that will keep you on the track; a guiding principle that you can live with to make sure you're consistent— and that your adversaries respect you for afterward.

The philosophy I suggest is very simple. I believe in winning at negotiations. But I also believe in winning by killing the opposition with kindness.

With kindness you win more for today, and more for tomorrow. In every negotiating situation you have a choice: You can act with kindness, or revert to characteristics common to lower creatures.

The word "negotiations" often has a negative connotation. When you read about people being "involved in negotiations," you often assume this indicates a mean, nasty, confrontational situation in which one person wins and the other loses. It is often *further* assumed that if you take a tough stance, act nasty and mean, you're more apt to be the winner. Corporate Darwinism—survival of the fittest—presupposes that only the toughest and most aggressive can win, that "nice guys finish last."

But aggressiveness *is not synonymous* with nastiness. To win at negotiations, you don't have to be a son of a bitch. If one party or the other could get what he wanted by *grabbing* it, there would be no bargaining. The very fact that you are involved in negotiations means that neither party is strong enough or secure enough to move independently, and so you try to arrange a *mutually satisfying outcome*. By the very act of sitting down, you imply that you will work something out. Remember, negotiating is a game. We all love to play games; it gives us a chance at self-expression, an opportunity to prove ourselves, to excel, to win—and, even when the goal is serious, to have a good time.

There is nothing wrong with having and using power with people—manipulating them. It's done all the time, and, in fact, it's the *only* way to get ahead. To me it's a question of *how* you choose to manipulate people. Do you leave your adversary hurt, shaken, embarrassed, intimidated? Or does the meeting end with a handshake and genuine goodwill?

The Weakness of Intimidation

You cannot influence people by bullying them. For the moment they may agree to what you impose on them, but all the time they seem to be doing what you want, they are seething, waiting, planning for revenge, which will ruin all you've gained. Winning by intimidation is a method with feet of clay, good for only *very* quick deals and transactions with people you'll never see again. (But how can you be sure? An old axiom says, "Friends may come and go, but enemies accumulate.") Winning with kindness is a method rooted in the very hearts of people—and lays a foundation you can always build on later.

No Need to Be Nasty

You wouldn't be negotiating if you didn't need some product or service and the person you are negotiating with didn't need some product or service from you. The goal of negotiations is for *both* sides to win, for everyone to get what he wants and compensate for it in a manner he can afford.

It's a waste of time and effort to get into a shouting match. People don't—*can't*—really listen or be logical when they are angry, screaming, and yelling at one another. Nor can they weigh new approaches or analyze subtle clues. (Why do you think professional chess matches are played in silence?) To negotiate quietly and calmly with kindness allows you to *listen and communicate*—without which the negotiations are stalled, mired in a flood of angry words.

The Futility of Anger

Anger is a red-hot "barrier" that closes off all avenues of negotiation. When you're angry, you can't think clearly. You focus on that one moment of irritation without perceiving the larger purpose of the negotiations. Anger also shows weakness: Not only are you unable to control the situation, but you are showing your frustration at not being able to control it *and get what you want easily*. To an opponent, anger reveals your momentary impotence—why put that kind of power in his hand?

If your opponent uses counterproductive tactics—such as being nasty, shaking, yelling, abusing and embarrassing people— don't take the bait. Why sink to his level? Just remember, he is not attacking *you;* he is trying to upset you so that you will make a mistake. You can't make a mistake as long as you fail to respond in kind and keep on broadcasting on *your* frequency.

Kindness Disarms Your Opponent

Most people enter negotiations ready to do battle. Many will attack you—shouting, screaming, thumping the table. If, on the other hand, their confrontational strategy makes no dent in you, your solid determination will throw them off their game plan. Now *they're* unprepared.

Just look what happened in the NFL players' strike. Ed Garvey, who represents the players, started the negotiations by name-calling, by putting down the owners' management council.

By getting the players revved up and excited, he got them into the name-calling act, and in the end they lost the negotiations.

The owners were determined; they stayed together and won.

Avoid Arrogance

You can always tell people they are wrong and demonstrate that you know all about them and have the goods on them. But what will that get you? You're not there to pin the other person to the wall, but to get something from him. You're not there to prove your experience or intelligence, but to get what you deserve.

Never Treat Your Opponent Like a Fool

If you think of the person confronting you as a sucker, you'll begin talking down to him, oversimplifying everything. You'll also be less guarded, less alert, and *you'll* come away with a foolish agreement that may not cover the points it should. Even if you really believe your opponent *is* a fool, don't treat him like one during a negotiation.

Why Argue?

Your opponent can't win an argument, and neither can you. Most arguments move away quickly from the substantive issues and deteriorate into personal attacks. You may walk away thinking you've won, but if you haven't gotten what you came to negotiate, you haven't won what you really deserve. And after most heated arguments, you've actually *lost* the chance to get it quickly and effectively.

Never Accuse

To let your opponent know he's wrong and that you have proof of it is not very smart. By saying things outright, you are going to wound your opponent's pride and get his back up. All *that* will accomplish is to arouse his basic instinct to defend himself, *right or wrong*.

You may give your ego a boost by this sort of one-upmanship, but what will it do for the negotiations? People resent being told they're wrong. Your opponent will fight back no matter what, and there won't be any further progress until he simmers down. And what will *that* loss of time and efficiency do for your pocketbook?

Never Corner Your Opponent

Corner someone only if you intend to kill him. But most negotiations are not life-or-death situations and cornering someone can be a terrible mistake. When they see there is no way out, people can get their backs up; and just to get out of that corner, they do crazy, harmful things both to themselves and to others.

The NFL Players Association cornered itself by saying it would take nothing less than 55 percent of the gross. It was "etched in stone." Nobody—or nobody who wants to win—uses that expression in negotiations. Only the names of the dead are etched in stone.

Never Close a Door

To say "Take it or leave it" is to end negotiations. Leave enough leeway for the other side to reconstruct the deal.

Kindness Is Decency

Winning should let you: (1) satisfy your needs (get what you deserve), but (2) remain true to what you are. Men are always talking about being able to look at themselves in the mirror when they shave. Well, acting decently, no matter what your opponent does, allows you to look at yourself, to be happy, and satisfied at having adhered to your highest standards.

You probably think of yourself as a kind person; almost everyone does. By winning through a strategy of kindness, you not only vindicate the goals you have set for the negotiations, but maintain your self-respect. And each time you win this way, you gain confidence, not only in the method, but in your own sense of who you are. With kindness as your delivery system, you do not feel any of the confusion or dishonesty or guilt that may make you pull back later.

Kindness Doesn't Mean Blandess or Ineffectuality

Many people confuse politeness and kindness with stepping back and letting someone get ahead of them, with lying down and letting someone walk all over them. That's not kindness, that's stupidity. Everyone is trying to get ahead, and there's nothing wrong with that—you should, too. But there are different ways of doing it; kindness is one way. The measure of a man or woman is expressed in his or her behavior toward others. In negotiations, to maintain the quality of kindness and *demonstrate* it to others is the most powerful tool you can possess. You can be tough, steadfast, strong, *and* kind, and lose nothing as long as you know what you want and are familiar with the techniques of negotiating. You don't have to play the macho game of trying to force others to do what you want. Only the weak and the unprepared *have* to be brutal, because they don't know any better ways to go about getting what they want. In negotiations your entire power lies in your position—who you are, the information you have, what you can offer the other side. Your effectiveness (which is not the same as your power) lies in knowing exactly what you want (ideally, this means having a clearer idea than your opponent, since clearer proposals always win over fuzzy ones). Thus prepared, you can adopt whatever particular negotiating tool and techniques the situation calls for, *but don't use them like a club to beat your counterpart into submission.*

Don't Ridicule People

Why put anyone down? If you push people into the ground and then stand on their shoulders, have you grown any taller? You gain nothing by standing on a fallen body!

Build *yourself* up by taking the negotiations to a higher level.

Kindness Is a Function of Security

If you know what *you* want, and why, then your negotiating position is already thought out by the time you sit down. You are ready with all the ammunition you'll need. Now, using politeness and diplomacy as "body English," you offer your opponent facts and figures, using the techniques you have learned to get your points across.

Your kindness both *guides and curbs* the power you possess. Instead of knocking over your opponent, you diplomatically demonstrate the error of his ways, and the correctness of your own.

Kindness is such a powerful weapon simply because people

can't *not* respond to it. Look at Rodney Dangerfield. Why is he so popular—and making all that money? What attracts people to him is his tag line, "I don't get no respect."

Rodney complains, "When I get sick, they give me second aid." He wants respect. *That's everybody's complaint.* Everyone wants others to look up to them, to respect them. By treating people with kindness and respect, you don't give up one iota of power. *You gain* by feeding into their craving for self-esteem.

Under all the huffing and puffing of the most belligerent negotiator is a desire to be respected. By treating that person with kindness, you are appealing to his most basic and, at the same time, his highest instinct. By touching that nerve you gain strength for your own negotiating positions; you have given your opponent the respect he craves and you have elevated yourself in his eyes. You have become a worthy opponent. More important, the esteem you have given him forces him to give you something in return—if not what you have been asking for, then at least equal politeness and consideration.

Negotiating Manners

How you choose to negotiate goes a long way in getting what you deserve. The manners you adopt determine the outcome; *you catch more flies with honey than with vinegar.*

Be polite: The old rules of manners are not only the easiest for most of us to use but get the best results. For example, pay attention to what is being said. By being polite enough to hear a person out from beginning to end, not only do you set the tone in the negotiations, but you wind up getting infinitely more information out of your opponent than if you keep interrupting him. The only way to be *sure* he's telling you all you need to hear is to let him talk. Negotiating from a position of kindness opens up unlimited avenues of communication.

Give people credit: Appreciate what people are. Why put them down? After all, they have something you want, and that commands respect. Make sure they *know* that you appreciate their importance. Remember, the person across from you is important right now if only because he or she has the ability to help you get what you deserve.

Don't condemn or find fault: Try to understand your opponent's position. By showing a sympathetic understanding, you need not give up anything. But your opponent will see you as someone who is aware of his problem. If you create empathy, he will come to look upon you as someone who can help him solve the problem. Instead of pointing out his faults, let him know that the two of you can work the problem out with mutual effort and understanding. To encourage his participation, tell him you have faith in his abilities to resolve the negotiations.

People want to deal with another human being they can trust. The world has become very cynical; yet down deep we all yearn for *trusting* relationships. We want others to trust us. So when you're negotiating, commit yourself in a positive way and deliver, even if it costs you at first. Once people begin to realize they can trust you, that you can fulfill commitments, you will begin building the trust that will help you get everything you deserve. As you work toward it, *it will come naturally.*

Don't you respond best to people who are positive, optimistic, *alive?* Sure you do! Tell stories, use humor, *share a little of yourself.* Presenting yourself in a warm, positive light motivates others to deal with you in the same fashion. If this deal doesn't work out, then there will be another one down the road. When you meet again, that person will remember you. And meanwhile you have gained valuable practice.

The secret is not in bragging but in presenting yourself as an alert, concerned, thoughtful person. Establish that kind of a relationship, and you can sell, buy, and negotiate any product, any service . . . *anything!*

CHAPTER
8

HACKSAW

A hulk of a man filled the screen of the TV monitor. Jack Reynolds, all 228 pounds of him, was standing in front of a bathroom door like a concrete Atlas, his shoulders wider than the door. He looked sweetly into the camera and said, "I'm a sensitive guy." His voice was light, pleasant. He half turned to open the door and took hold of the knob with his huge paw. With no apparent effort, he yanked the door off its hinges. Holding the door up in the air as if it were an attaché case, he turned back to the camera. His clear blue eyes twinkling, his light brown mustache twitching, he shrugged his shoulders.

"Cut," called the director of the commercial. He peered around from behind the camera, looking at Jack, and his thumb and forefinger came together forming a circle. "That was really good, guys," he announced to everyone on the set. "Now, Jack, we're going to do it again. This time, though,"—the director's voice was soothing, stroking—"let's have more of a shit-eating grin on your face."

Jack had no trouble with what the director wanted. All he had to do was think about what had happened in the past eighteen months.

Jack "Hacksaw" Reynolds is still one of the great middle linebackers in pro football, but in 1980 he was getting very little for his efforts. He was thirty-two years old and had been playing foot-

163

ball since he was eight. For six months out of the year, Jack thought, talked, ate, slept, and dreamed football, twenty-four hours a day. The Los Angeles Rams' 1979 media guide said: "For nine NFL seasons, Jack Reynolds has contributed greatly to the success of the Rams . . ." The 1980 media guide applauded Reynolds as being the "All-Pro" player who "led" and "directed" the powerful and very effective Rams' defense.

But when it came down to negotiate a new contract, Hacksaw couldn't get the Rams' management to translate his time, skills, and leadership into money.

Jack had used an attorney to negotiate his contracts. In 1980 he was earning $125,000 a year, with all but $30,000 deferred for seven years. By anybody's measure, he was getting a raw deal. When I started representing Jack, I got John Shaw to agree to release the deferred payments.

The year 1980 was Hacksaw's option year. This, he believed, was the year he was going to collect on all the promises the club had made over the years. During the season the Rams kept making promises on a new contract: a bigger salary, a no-cut clause, and bonuses.

After the season in early 1981, Jack went in to see Don Klosterman, the Rams' general manager, to nail all those promises down. Jack thought all he had to do was repeat what they had agreed to: "You promised me a three-year guarantee and a no-cut contract."

Klosterman looked away from Jack, focusing on a far corner of the room. "I'm sorry," Klosterman said, now looking back at Jack. "All I can offer you is a two-year contract, with no guarantees."

Translated, that meant if Jack didn't make the team, bye-bye and no salary. The Rams had gone back on every promise they had made.

The blood rushed to Jack's head. His face was frozen, his voice ice cold. "That's unfair, Don."

Klosterman looked straight at Reynolds. "That's all we can offer you, Jack. You gotta remember, you're going to be thirty-four."

The Rams' management was looking at the wrong numbers— not at what Jack had accomplished but what was left in him. It didn't matter that he had been a regular for eight years. It didn't matter he had made more tackles than any other defensive player on the Rams. Only his age mattered. And Jack knew management was misjudging him. He had three or four good years left in him.

Jack's eyes were full of rage, his fists clenched so tight his nails threatened to cut the palms of his hands. He had to get out of there or he would level Klosterman. Slowly, controlling himself, he got up and went to the door.

Behind his back he heard the GM say, "Oh, one thing, Jack. We need an answer in forty-eight hours."

Jack left Anaheim Stadium, got into his Jeep, and drove straight to his in-laws in Chattanooga, Tennessee. He drove without stopping, except for gas. It was that same determined concentration that got him his nickname, "Hacksaw," when he was with Tennessee in 1969. That was the year they went to play Ole Miss, and if they won the game, they were going to the Sugar Bowl. But Tennessee, which had won the Southeast Conference, lost to Mississippi 38–0.

The team came back to Tennessee a tired, unhappy bunch of guys. The next day Jack spotted a 1953 Chevy that was considered a school mascot—it was little more than a battered frame that was constantly being pushed from one end of the campus to the other. Why, he doesn't know, perhaps to relieve the frustration he felt, but Jack started sawing the Chevy in half. At one point the car began to sag, but he was determined to cut it in half. He got some beams to boost it up. It took him eight hours and thirteen hacksaw blades from K mart to cut the car right through the drive shaft. By the next day the two halves of the car had disappeared. But Jack had earned his name, and it's been part of him ever since.

By the time Jack got to Chattanooga, he had cooled off. He realized he was too personally involved with the Rams to do well for himself. He and I had talked before this when I was representing Ferragamo. Jack had had several bad experiences with agents and didn't like them. "Most disappear after you sign a contract. You never see them and you never hear from them." But since Jack was a powerful and important part of the Rams' defense, and Vince an important part of the Rams' offense, I felt it would be a conflict to represent both players at the same time because if I got a lot of money for one player, the team would expect me to take less on the other.

The day after Vince signed with the Alouettes, Jack called me and asked me to represent him. I telephoned the Rams, who of course were not too happy to hear from me again, and asked to open negotiations. What Klosterman said floored me: "We're going to release Jack, outright."

"*Release him?*" I couldn't believe it. "But Don, what about all that talk you gave me with Vince? What did you say? 'Players get more money when they're over the hill than when they're ascending. Money is paid for past services and contributions.' And Jack isn't over the hill. He's in his prime!"

"David, all I can tell you is we are going to release Jack."

It was crazy. Who ever released a pro bowl linebacker without asking for compensation?

"Oh, David," Klosterman said. "Will you do me a favor? Tell Jack."

"*Me?*" Suddenly I felt like I had put my hand in a hornet's nest. "Don't make me a hatchet man. I'm calling to negotiate. If you don't want to negotiate, then *you* call Jack yourself and tell him what you're going to do. You owe him an explanation; he's given you the best years of his life."

Klosterman had Rams' coach, Ray Malavasi, call Jack, but he beat around the bush and never actually told him what they were going to do.

Jack read about his future—or lack of it—in the papers the next day. He was hurt and angry. What upset him the most was the way they did it—after eleven years, an outright release that branded him a washup. It was as if the Rams were saying, "He's not worth anything." Why would any club release a Jack Reynolds? Did the Rams know something about his physical condition? They were certainly sending a negative signal out to all the other clubs.

It was left to me to smooth out the damage. We soft-pedaled the release, but, in fact, the outright release had given me a very good negotiating position. Clubs aren't used to dealing with a truly free agent of Jack's capacity. Usually when a guy is released on waivers, he *is* washed up or has had a bad year. But here was a man running at the peak of his performance. The only compensation the Rams had given Jack for all his years was an advantage in negotiating with the other teams. He was free and clear to go to any other club.

The minute the news was out, club offers poured in. Five were very firm: San Diego, Buffalo, Philadelphia, San Francisco, and Chicago. Jack and I sat down and reviewed which ones would benefit the most from his skills. Who was in need of a middle linebacker? I had told all the GM's that Jack would have to visit them, talk to the coaches, find out the types of defenses they were planning to use—in a word, to see how much playing time he would be given.

Clubs could make their decisions on Jack's skills and his skills alone. They wouldn't have to see what it would cost them in compensation or draft picks—all of which would make him a much more expensive player. So we set up a schedule to visit all the clubs that had come in with offers. Immediately we discovered which ones were seriously interested—those which had Jack fly first class instead of coach, the ones that picked him up at the airport instead of telling him to hop into a cab and come over. It was easy to tell which clubs treated Jack like the superstar he was; and from their attitude toward him, I knew what leverage I had with each of them.

Even though my talks with the Buffalo Bills were progressing to a final stage, Buffalo was the only place Jack didn't visit. Jack already knew the Bills' coach, Chuck Knox, who had been with the Rams for five years. I went to Buffalo, and we came to a financial arrangement.

Then suddenly the Oakland Raiders got interested, as did the San Diego Chargers. I spoke several times to Jack Teele in San Diego. Teele, too, had been with the Rams, so Jack knew him well. But the best offer had come from Buffalo, and we planned a trip up there.

Jack came into New York on a Wednesday night. That day I leaked a story that Jack was leaning toward the Bills and would likely sign with them. I also let it be known we were going to Buffalo. The next morning before eleven o'clock New York time, I got a call from John McVay of the San Francisco 49ers. He and the coach, Bill Walsh, wanted Reynolds.

I listened, and had to weigh my words very carefully. Jack would love to play for the 49ers, feeling he could make a bigger impact if he signed with a club that wasn't doing too well. Walsh's offense wasn't a problem; he had that solid. But the 49ers' defense was hurting, and they knew it. For the secondary, they had drafted a bunch of young guys who could learn. When Jack and I reviewed the 49ers, he said, "I can show those people how to win."

He could, but he had to get paid for it. "Look," I told McVay, "Jack would like to play in San Francisco, but I can't recommend the deal you're offering. If you want Jack to play for you, you gotta come up with more money."

"I'll call you back," McVay said.

"Okay, but we're heading for Buffalo on the one o'clock flight from La Guardia."

At 11:30, I left my office with Jack. I told my secretary I had to stop at Artie Moskowitz's office at the William Morris Agency to collect a check for an act.

The Morris agency is only three blocks from my office, and when I arrived, there was a message for me: "Call your office." I discovered that McVay wanted to speak to me right away.

When I got McVay on the line he said, "We want Jack Reynolds."

"Okay, here's what we want: a three-year contract, a million dollars, and a guaranteed no-cut clause."

McVay didn't say anything, so I added, "Jack likes the Forty-niners, but he's going out to Buffalo to give them [the Bills] a fair chance."

"I'll call you back in five minutes," said McVay.

Five minutes later, McVay did call. I told him I wanted to put him on the speaker phone. "Jack is with me. I want him to hear." McVay agreed. I sat across from Jack, watching his face as I took notes.

McVay offered $500,000.

I repeated my demands for a million.

Back and forth we went until we settled on $848,000, on a three-year contract with an option year; plus the team would insure the contract against injury. That meant that if Jack was injured, he would still get paid whether he played or not.

Once we agreed on that, we negotiated bonuses for team wins, tackles, and All-Pro selection.

A broad smile broke out on Jack's face and I agreed.

By the time we got done, it was 12:15. I told McVay to send me the contract. Jack was nervous about Buffalo, but I told him we were still going. "We have to. We told them we'll be there and we're gonna show up."

We caught a cab on Sixth Avenue. As usual, I told the driver, "There's an extra five bucks if you get us to La Guardia in twenty minutes." As we raced across town, Jack asked me, "What are we going to tell them in Buffalo?"

"Don't worry," I replied. "I got us into this. I'll get you out of it."

"What are you going to say?"

"Let me think."

The Bills picked us up at the airport, and we went into a meeting with Stu Barber, their general manager. All the while, I was thinking of the San Francisco offer. The 49ers and the Rams are in the same division. They play each other twice during the regular season. Jack would give anything for a chance at them. I had to get out of the Buffalo deal.

Before I brought up money or let Barber mention it, I said, "Stu, it's important there be a good rapport between Jack and the coaching staff. Can Chuck Knox join us before we make a deal?"

"Sure, David." Barber called Knox, and a few minutes later he joined us. Everyone said hello. It was obvious that Jack and Chuck got along. They talked football, about the old times together, about how they were going to bring good times to Buffalo.

Before they got into a kissing match, I interrupted, "Chuck? What are your plans for Jack?"

Normally, it isn't the agent's role to question a coach about how he will use a player. Football coaches are autocrats. They don't even like to answer to their general managers, let alone an agent. Most coaches believe agents know nothing about football, and if you ask them to spell things out, they get angry as hell.

Knox moved his chair away from Jack and faced me. I could see he was angry. "This is a tough organization. We got a lot of good talent here. Jack will just have to come in like everyone else, and try to make the club."

I had to heat things up a little, so I raised my voice. Looking straight at Knox, I said, "When Sinatra goes to Las Vegas, does he have to audition?"

The veins on Knox's temples started bulging. He remained

calm, but his voice had lost all of its friendliness. "Buffalo is not Las Vegas. We're not gambling here. And Jack Reynolds isn't Sinatra."

Stu Barber saw what was happening. He didn't know why I was doing this, but he could guess. He wanted Jack on his club and didn't want the deal to sour. "I think Jack should talk to Chuck alone." Stu got up and gestured for me to go with him.

We left them alone. As soon as we got into the hall, Stu said, "You bastard. What do you have, a better deal?"

"No," I said, keeping a straight face. "I don't think Jack has to try out for anything."

In a few minutes Jack and Chuck came out and the meeting was over. We agreed to talk the next day. Jack and I went back to New York. The next day's headlines read: HACKSAW MAY END UP IN BILLS' TOOL CHEST. All the world thought that Jack Reynolds was signing with the Buffalo Bills. The same afternoon, I got the contract from San Francisco. Jack and I went over it. It had everything we had asked for, and Jack signed it.

The story doesn't end there. Jack went to San Francisco, all fired up to play football. The 49ers were coming off three lousy years of 2 and 14, 2 and 14, and 6 and 10. They had never seen anyone like Jack; he was going to bring them a winning attitude. The younger ballplayers and the rookies watched the way he practiced, the way he studied. At thirty-four he was the old man on the team but the youngest in spirit and optimism. They were amazed, because with his skill and record, Jack didn't have to prove anything. He was out to show them that skill and *inspiration* make great football players.

The 49ers played the Rams twice, beating them both times—once in San Francisco and once in Los Angeles. When Jack Reynolds took the field in Anaheim Stadium, he got a standing ovation from the fans. It pleased him, but it was also a little sad. In an interview he said, "I got more recognition [in San Francisco] in a quarter of a year than I did in L.A. in eleven years. I just feel good. I've been reborn here."

No one, not even the 49ers themselves, expected them to be contenders in '81. They were building a team; management was content to win and gain experience. But the players were fired up. Maybe it was because they beat their archrivals twice; maybe it was the inspiration of Jack Reynolds. They charged through the season, through the play-offs, into the Super Bowl, and opened up a 20–7 lead over the Cincinnati Bengals.

But then suddenly, late in the third quarter, the momentum started changing. The Bengals moved down the field and had the ball on the three-yard line. It was first-and-goal. The Bengals had four plays to score. Everyone was certain they would; this would shift the game to them.

On the first down, 249-pound Pete Johnson slammed into the line. He gained two yards. It was second-and-one from the one-yard line. Johnson hit the left side. This was the Bengals' power play, their money play over Anthony Munoz and Dave Lapham behind running back Charles Alexander. Johnson had over 800 pounds in front of him. The 49er line was being hit by over a thousand pounds of power. The 49er defense closed the hole, and Jack Reynolds, coming in over the top, smashed into Johnson, hitting him high, stopping him dead in his tracks, making what was called the play of the game. *No gain.*

It was third-and-one. The Bengals were stopped again at the one on a roll-out pass to Alexander. Fourth-and-one. Johnson followed Alexander into the hole. What hole? San Francisco had ten men on the line and, led by Jack Reynolds, cut Johnson down at the line of scrimmage.

A jubilant 49er defense came off the field, their feet hardly touching the ground. They knew they were going to win Super Bowl XVI. Hacksaw had been waiting years for this; he was finally getting what he deserved.

In football (and in many companies), after you've put in ten years or more, you're earning a darn good salary. Then someone who is cost-conscious says he can cut the cost in half by hiring a younger person to do the same job. Your employers don't look at what you've contributed, or care how much you still have to contribute. They add up the numbers, and say, "Good-bye."

Jack was lucky in that he got a chance to show the Rams how wrong they were.

Don't Take It Personally

Jack had been doing his own negotiating with the Rams. When they wouldn't give him what he wanted and demanded, he took it personally because he felt he had a close relationship with the team.

That was a mistake. One of the problems when people negotiate for themselves is that they tend to take things personally. But no matter what the relationships are in a business situation, it's still business. Whatever happens, look at it from a business point of view. You must always *expect* situations that may be distasteful to you but that are a part of business.

Deadlines

Again, Jack had great confidence in himself. He was certain he would find a linebacker position on any team. He knew the Rams needed him, so when they gave him a deadline, he didn't buy it.

You have to be careful when people set deadlines. If someone says, for example, "We need an answer in forty-eight hours," this can mean one of two things. First, the negotiator may be using a scare tactic; he wants to fluster you, to make you panic and *not* think. But on the other hand, there *are* valid considerations of time. For instance, a team may need an answer before it goes into a draft and needs to know what positions are open. In a case like that, a deadline is a legitimate request. But when a team slaps a deadline on a player for no apparent reason, just because it feels like getting things over with, that means it wants to put the pressure on.

For either side, a deadline can be a very useful tool. If you have several job opportunities, a deadline can help you make your choice. If you tell all your prospective employers that you need an answer within a certain amount of time, then the person who responds fastest will be the one who wants you the most.

It may be that you really *don't* need to know in a specific period of time. That doesn't matter. Perhaps you actually have a week or two in which to make a decision; but keep your time frame to yourself.

Read the Signs

People tend to give themselves away, but most of us are so busy with ourselves we don't see what others are "saying." As an agent, I can sit back and watch what is happening. With the teams that claimed they wanted Jack Reynolds, I was very careful to watch how they treated him. From their initial contact, the 49ers treated Jack not only as the star he was, but as someone *they wanted*. Beyond all their words and actions lay the strong desire to add Jack to their team.

How you're treated, how you're spoken to, the kind of atmosphere around a negotiation should tell you if you're wanted or not. All you have to do is look for the signs, read them, and negotiate accordingly.

Use the Experts

One reason why Jack Reynolds is a sensational client is because he *uses* me as his agent. Because he regards me as an expert at what I do, he listens to my advice.

There have been a lot of cases in which players have been taken by their agents. But there are an awful lot more players and personalities who have listened to their agents and attorneys, and have come out ahead.

Use an expert who not only knows how to negotiate, but is aware of what's going on in your field. The expert should be aware of the compensation offered in salary *and* in the perks that people in your position are offered in other companies.

If you're going to hire an expert, let him do the job that he or she is an expert at. If you're going to second-guess a negotiator, then why have an agent working for you? Jack and I have been successful together because he does his business and I do mine. He believes he's a pro at what he does on the field, and that I'm a pro in my business. And Jack's confidence motivates me to get him more work: I go out and bust my tail to prove he's right to place his trust in me. *That* is the ideal working relationship.

Are You Weighing All the Options?

Whatever you're negotiating for, weigh it against the alternatives. In Jack's case other considerations were involved besides which city to play in and the money. When the choice came between San Francisco and Buffalo, Jack listed all the positive and negative aspects of both cities. On the positive side, Jack liked San Francisco. San Francisco played on grass, and he believed his legs would last longer on grass than on Astroturf. He thought the

49ers were a young team and he knew the division very well. Always having been a West Coast player, he was used to the weather.

In many cases the money will outweigh all other considerations, but be sure to look at them anyway. After all, you are working to enjoy a certain life-style. If you live where you can't have that life-style, what good is the money?

Homework

Once Jack knew the Rams were going to release him, he and I sat down and went over all the possible places he could play. We investigated the cities where Jack could live and the linebacker positions on those clubs. There was no sense even considering places Jack didn't want to live in, or where his talents would not be used and needed. Even if one of these clubs had come in with a money offer, we would have rejected it. Once we knew where Jack would make a contribution, we were able to begin serious negotiations.

Doing your homework is very important, and it pays off. Mike Leventhal is a WABC-TV producer. When he was an ABC reporter, his job was to find out what was going on in the sports scene. When he went in to negotiate a salary, he brought all his files with him and said, "Here are the stories I've broken. Here's why I deserve a raise."

Todd Christenson called me for advice regarding his upcoming negotiations with Al Davis. Todd was the captain of the special team unit during the Raiders' win at the Super Bowl in 1981, and then he went on to lead the team in pass receptions as a tight end. I was amazed to see him pull out a list of his specific involvements in each of the last twenty wins of the Raiders. Whether it was a fumble recovery that led to the winning touchdown, an interception that stopped a drive, or a touchdown reception from Jim Plunkett that won a game, every detail was included in his list.

Getting Out of a Deal

In every situation it's important to leave yourself an out. Whether you say you're in a rush now and can't decide, or blame it on your wife, husband, or some other party, always have an out,

so that if and when you go back to negotiate with people, they
don't get mad at you.

In Buffalo I knew that Chuck Knox didn't want any agent telling him where Jack Reynolds should play. I felt in my heart that
was the wrong question to ask a coach, but I also knew it would be
the perfect opening wedge to break off the negotiations. I was
sure Chuck would take offense at my question, and he did—
enough to make sure that nothing got settled in Buffalo.

It's important to find out your opponent's weakness, the point
at which he'll lose his temper. I don't mean, hit him below the
belt; that's no good. But when you know a person's weakness, you
are one up in a negotiation.

CHAPTER

9

ENDORSEMENTS

Tony Sciametta's company is a Wall Street firm of foreign-exchange traders. One reason the firm grew so fast in a short period of time was the *point of identity* Tony created for the company, an identity bankers and their families wanted to be associated with.

One day Tony got a call from a woman complaining that he'd been keeping her husband out four nights a week. "He never gets home before four in the morning." The woman started crying. "Why do you have to take him out every night?" she wailed. "You're taking him away from his family."

Tony heard the woman out. When she was done and had finally stopped, he said, "I haven't done business with your husband in half a year."

Obviously Tony was being used as an excuse for an errant husband. But the experience taught him a valuable lesson, and he started gearing the entertainment of clients—mostly bankers—to a more family-oriented style. Instead of taking them out to shows, dinners, nightclubs, he organized sports events they could participate in and *show off* to their families.

One night, I arranged for Earl Monroe, Phil Esposito, Ron Duguay, Lou Piniella, Drew Pearson, Toby Knight, John Havlicek, Burgess Owens, and Mickey Rivers to play basketball with Tony's clients. They played at the Regina Youth Center in Brooklyn, and

I even hired Warner Wolf, a gregarious local New York television sportscaster, to announce the players onto the court and do the play-by-play over the loudspeaker.

The idea was a tremendous success. Under every three-piece gray suit is a jock, and what greater fantasy could a man have than playing with superstars? Whether the guy was taking a pass from Earl the Pearl or driving past Hondo for a lay-up, his family was in the stands watching it happen, hearing it announced. And we had several photographers around to make sure the event was recorded for posterity. I also once arranged a baseball game for Tony's clients that included Mickey Mantle, Whitey Ford, and Willie Mays, among others.

Well, one day early in my career, I got a call from Tony. He wanted a basketball player for a luncheon his company was having. "David," he said, "get whoever you want. I leave it to you."

I tried to think of a truly *impressive* basketball player, and one man came to mind immediately: John Havlicek. When I was a kid growing up in the Boston area, the only basketball team we ever spoke about was the Celtics. John Havlicek was my idol. What inspired me was that as the sixth man, John always came off the bench, gave his all, and wound up a winner. Now suddenly I had a chance to meet him—or at least an excuse to talk to him.

I called Larry Fleischer, John's attorney. Larry is also the attorney for the NBA Players Association. He had been very helpful when I was just starting to promote basketball stars for summer camps.

Larry gave me John's unlisted home phone number. I called, introduced myself, and asked if he would be interested in a personal appearance in New York.

"Sure," he said in his flat midwestern accent.

John came into New York, went to the luncheon, made a speech, and signed autographs. Everybody loved him.

That evening John and I had dinner together, and he told me a story that puts idol worship in perspective. As you might imagine, he and his son, John, Jr., go to a lot of Celtics games. One day his son said to him, "Daddy, can you introduce me to Larry Bird?"

After the game John took his son to the locker room and introduced him to Larry Bird. Larry shook hands with the kid and signed an autograph for him. On the way out, John Jr., held up his hand and showed it to his father—one of the greatest basketball players who ever lived—and said, "I'm never going to wash this hand. It shook Larry Bird's."

After dinner I walked John to the Plaza Hotel where I had gotten him a suite, and we said good night. For me it had been a great day.

A few days later I got a thank-you note from John Havlicek. It enclosed his business card, and in the note he wrote that if I was ever in the neighborhood, I should call and we would have a meal together. I was so honored I had the letter framed and put it up on my office wall.

Three years later I got a call from Syd Rangel at Needham, Harper, and Steers, an advertising agency. Xerox was promoting a small office machine, and the point of the commercial was that even though Xerox is a huge corporation, it can also cater to the small-business man. To dramatize this concept, they wanted a tall, oldtime basketball player to get up and say, "Hi. I'm a small-business man . . ."

As I was listening to Syd telling me about the campaign, my eyes went to John's letter on the wall facing me.

"Who do you have in mind?" I asked.

Syd mentioned a name—a ballplayer who was doing ads for a local muffler dealer.

"Is he interested?" I asked.

"We haven't asked him, but I'm sure he'll do it for us." His tone was unmistakably, *This is for Xerox. Who would turn them down?*

"But is that what you really want? Do you want Xerox identified as being in the same league as a muffler company?" You see, one of my jobs for many major corporations is to match the athlete with the product. It's much more than having an athlete say he uses a product, or what have you. It's a question of image identification—of which athlete would be the most successful for the particular product.

There was a silence on the other end of the phone, so I said quickly, "Have you thought of John Havlicek?"

"No."

"You know, he *is* a small-business man. He has a Wendy's franchise."

I could almost hear Syd thinking. "Have you ever met him?" I asked.

"No. We're not meeting anyone just now. We're selecting from stock photos, and then we'll do a test on whomever we choose."

"How about if I ask John to come in and see you?" I was sure that if the agency people met him in person, they would like him.

"Can't afford it," Syd said. "It's not in our budget."

"Okay. I'll get on to some basketball players, and give you a call in a day or two."

I immediately called John, told him what Xerox had in mind, and suggested it would be worth his while to come to New York and meet the agency people. "It'll have to be at your own expense," I added. "But it'll put you miles ahead of anyone else they're considering."

John was interested, but now I had to be sure of *his* image. "John, do you have any misdemeanors?"

"No, David." He understood what I was getting at. "But I'll tell you a funny story. After one NBA championship the TV people and photographers crowded into the dressing room, and of course we were pouring champagne over each other and guzzling from the bottle. Everyone saw it. For months I kept getting calls and letters from priests and rabbis throughout the country saying, 'You're John Havlicek. What kind of image are you giving our children, drinking champagne on television?' Since then I've been very careful with my image."

John came to New York at a meeting I set up with the agency. He is an extremely cordial, articulate, personable man with a charming smile, and Syd and the agency were very impressed. They set up a TV and print-ad test, and even suggested that John go up to Rochester and meet the Xerox people handling the campaign.

John went to Rochester, and I got a call as he was waiting for a plane back to Boston that evening. "David," he said, "they want me to do several personal appearances for them at a convention in Atlanta."

"What did you say?" I was elated with John's news. It meant Xerox wanted him to represent them. It meant they would want him for the commercial. It also meant I could go into Needham, Harper, and Steers and make a good deal; Xerox was already committed.

"I told them I would do it and for them to work the details out with you."

There are two very important lessons here. One is that John killed me with kindness. His thank-you note was a gracious gesture. He didn't have to do it. Most others don't. He did it because that's the sort of person he is. It made a lasting impression on me, an impression that not only made me like him more, but earned him some money because he was the first one I thought of when I was asked to provide a basketball player.

The second lesson is simply never to put your cards on the table while you're still negotiating. The minute Xerox asked John to go to Atlanta as *their representative*, they allowed me to go into the ad agency with a full house. It wasn't that I could hold them up; it was that I knew he was wanted and therefore I was able to get the best price for my client because I knew Xerox had already committed themselves.

Image *is* important. This is why for many years hockey players were rarely seen doing advertisements on television. Because of the level of violence of the sport, many parents didn't like their children watching hockey games, and so many sponsors wouldn't use hockey players. But several years ago, four hockey players swept the commercial field.

What happened was that Audrey Nizen, former vice-president of advertising at Sasson Jeans, was a big hockey fan and decided to use players in a commercial. She got four of the New York Rangers—Phil Esposito, Ron Duguay, Dave Maloney, and Ulf Nilsson—to wear Sasson jeans and skate around Madison Square Garden with the "Oo-la-la, Sasson" tune playing behind them.

I got involved because at that time I was one of Phil Esposito's agents, along with Fred Scharf in Boston. Phil is one of the all-time great hockey players—first with the Boston Bruins and then with the New York Rangers. Now retired, Esposito is a sportscaster for CBS-TV and a local New York cable station that carries the Rangers' games.

Phil was told he would be paid $5,000, but the Sasson Jeans

people didn't want any agents involved. I didn't have a written contract with Phil. He didn't have to call me about the spot. But he did, and I appreciated his honesty. He wanted to do the commercial, but he knew he couldn't get it if I got involved. I told him to go ahead and do it, and not worry about me—I thought it would be great for him and it might be a chance to get more hockey players to do commercials.

As you may recall, the commercial turned out to be an incredible success. Audrey had the idea at the right time: The United States hockey team had just won the Olympics, and the fact that the four Rangers were wearing jeans and not their regular uniforms softened the hockey image.

One night as I was watching the commercial, Monica turned to me and asked, "David, wouldn't it be great if you could do a commercial like this with four New York Yankees?"

"Monica, I'd love to. But the woman at Sasson doesn't like to use agents. She wouldn't want to do business with me."

Monica gave me a funny look and said no more. But she had planted an idea in my head. Now it was a challenge. By the time I got to the office the next day, I was trying to figure out a way to wangle a Sasson commercial for Lou Piniella.

Actually I wanted that commercial for Lou because I believe one of the best ways to motivate a ballplayer is by having his face on the tube. He plays better and he puts out a little extra because he now feels he's also representing a major corporation.

I knew Lou had made plans to come to New York the next day. I had set up a personal appearance for the following night at the Lincoln Savings Bank. So that morning I called Sasson and asked for Audrey Nizen.

When she got on the phone, I said, "Hi, I'm Lou Piniella," doing my great imitation of Lou's voice, getting that deep southern accent of his that's so distinctive.

"I see your commercials all the time"—I paused to see if she was listening. No sounds from the other end, so I went on—"I think it would be a great idea to use me and three other teammates in your commercial."

"Are you really Lou Piniella?" Audrey exclaimed.

"Sure, I'm Lou Piniella."

I could hear the excitement in her voice. "When can you come in and see me?"

"Well, I live in Florida, but I happen to be in town for a few days. I can see you tomorrow anytime."

"Come in at eleven A.M."

"Okay, see you then."

Even before hanging up the phone, I realized I had a problem. Lou was coming in at 1:30 the next day. I immediately rang up Lou in Florida.

"Lou," I said in my Lou Piniella voice, "you have to come into New York early tomorrow. Take the seven o'clock plane."

Lou sometimes laughs when I imitate his voice, but today all he said was, "Why?"

"Just take the plane."

"What's it all about, David?"

"Trust me, it's something good. Can't you trust a man who talks this way?"

We both laughed, and Lou promised to be on that plane. Sure enough, he came off the Delta flight at 9:30.

He had had to wake up at five o'clock to catch that plane, and his eyes bore into me. "What's up, David? It'd better be good."

"Lou, don't get angry at me, but you know how I love to imitate your voice all the time . . ." And then I told him what I did. He started roaring; he couldn't believe it! But he was ready to play along.

One of the things Audrey had said to "Lou" over the phone was "I hope you don't have an agent." I answered, "No." So Lou and I worked out a story: I would go along with him—not as his agent, but as his partner in the baseball camp we have, and I *just* happened to be with him today.

We went to the meeting with Audrey and the Sasson president, Paul Guez. During the meeting Audrey said she'd been thinking of using Bucky Dent. But there had been a lot of hassling between her and Bucky's agent. She turned to Lou and said, "I hate dealing with agents. But if you hadn't called, I probably would have used a guy on the Red Sox."

In those days everybody wanted to do a Sasson Jeans commercial, so the Sasson people had a very strong negotiating position.

Basically, the company felt it had a hot product and it could control the dollars it was offering. From my point of view and from Lou's, the commercial would be great exposure for him. There was no question in my mind that once the commercial came out he would be more valuable as a spokesman, and we could raise Lou's personal appearance fee from $500 to $1,500 a night.

In ten minutes we made a deal to everyone's liking, a deal so successful it lasted for two years.

The commercial was shot in California: Lou Piniella playing baseball with six top models, including Suzy Coleo, who was Sonny Bono's girl friend at the time. I have to give Audrey a lot of credit because the campaign generated more excitement than any other I've seen. The commercial was very popular; Sasson got a lot of publicity, and Lou's face was seen across the country.

The logistics in getting to California the day of the shoot was a bit of a trick. There was a Friars' Roast for George Steinbrenner that afternoon in New York. I had arranged for Lou to be the first speaker. As soon as he got done, I rushed him out; I wouldn't even let him stay for the applause.

I had a car waiting to take us to Kennedy Airport. I wasn't sure we could make our flight, so I called my secretary as we raced across Queens and asked her to make alternate reservations if we missed the flight we were booked on. When we got to TWA, the plane was still at the gate. I couldn't believe it. We were late—a good seven minutes—but the plane was waiting for us. I don't know what my secretary did, but she must have done some fancy negotiating to get TWA to delay a takeoff.

I later admitted what I had done and wrote Audrey a five-page apology explaining that perhaps she had had some bad experiences, but not *all* agents are bad people. I had done it because the word was out that she was dead set against agents, and this was the only possible way I could get the job for my client. I wanted the job for him because I knew Lou and Sasson would be a terrific combination.

Audrey gave me a call to say she accepted my apology. "All right, David, you delivered. Now get me a quarterback!"

"Would you like Vince Ferragamo?"

"Whatever . . . just so he's a quarterback. Is Vince a quarterback?"

Even today I don't know if she knew who Vince Ferragamo was, that he was my client—or if she was just being very smart. Her attitude was *I just want a quarterback.*

"I'll get him for you. When are you shooting?"

"Thursday morning." She paused. This was Monday afternoon. "Can I count on you?"

At this time I didn't even go through the numbers with her. It was a chance at a solid national commercial for Vince—the first one that wasn't all talk. It would build a profile for him that could only get him other commercials. "It's a deal. You'll have him."

Except that I had no idea where Vince was. I called Jodi in California. "Vince is at some football camp. I don't remember its name, and he told me the number, but I didn't write it down."

Swell. I had a commercial to be shot in New York in three days.

"I remember the area code though," said Jodi. "It's nine one six."

I knew that most of the football camps are located in small towns. So I called the operator and asked for the names of twenty-five small cities in the 916 code area. Then I started calling all the police chiefs in these towns, figuring that if someone like Vince Ferragamo was in their areas, they would know. Sure enough, about three quarters through my list, a guy said, "Yeah. He's working at the local camp."

It had taken me a full day to track him down, but on Tuesday night I had him on the phone. "Vince," I said, "you gotta catch a plane tomorrow to be here Thursday morning. We got a commercial to shoot."

"David," Vince sighed, "how can I leave here? The day after the Super Bowl I made a commitment to the owner. He's an old friend."

"Put him on the phone." When he got on, I said, "I have a very important opportunity for Vince in New York on Thursday. Would it be okay to replace him with another NFL player?"

"Sure," the guy replied.

"I'll get back to you."

I called Wendell Tyler, a running back for the Rams. He agreed to go and replace Vince at the camp.

Vince flew in on the "Red Eye." I picked him up Thursday morning, and we drove straight to Columbia University's Baker

Field at 210th Street. Vince had left San Francisco at ten o'clock the night before and flown all night. He had had three hours of sleep, but he's a pro; a couple of cups of coffee and he was ready to go.

The shot was with six girls—models. They lined up, all wearing Sasson jeans, and the "Oo-la-la" song was playing in the background. The girls were ready to snap the ball to Vince, their little tushes all moving to the beat of the music.

Vince started to call out the signals. "Huut . . . huut . . . forty-eight—twelve—"

"Hey, Vince," one of the Sasson guys interrupted. "Why don't you use thirty-six . . . twenty-two . . . thirty-six?"

I looked at Audrey. "That's not right, Audrey."

Audrey's nose went up. "Sexist!" And we did the commercial using the *real numbers:* "Twenty-two . . . forty-eight . . . huut . . . huut . . ."

Vince made sure every Rams player got a pair of jeans and a sweatshirt when the team came to New York. This piece of generosity apparently paid off: That Sunday he went out and threw four touchdown passes, and the Rams scored forty-four points.

Both commercials made my clients, Lou Piniella and Vince Ferragamo, more marketable because they had gotten a female audience rather than the jock crowd for most sports commercials.

You hear a lot about athletes doing a thirty-second or a one-minute commercial and laughing all the way to the bank. Well, some do. After all, athletes are human beings, and it's human nature to search for the fast buck. But there's another part of human nature athletes possess, one that rarely gets public notice.

I got a call from Gloria Gengo at Needham, Harper, and Steers. The commercial they wanted to do was terrific. They wanted Roger Staubach to put a drawing of a football into a Xerox machine on one coast and have Drew Pearson "catch" it from an identical machine on the other coast—and the whole process would take seconds.

I called Roger. He liked the idea and also liked doing a commercial for Xerox, but when I told him how much they would pay—$30,000 for him, $20,000 for Drew—he hesitated.

"If you're interested," I said, "I think we can get more. You let me know. I won't call Drew until you decide."

Roger said very insistently, "If I'm going to do it, I'll call Drew."

Two days later, Roger called. "David, I'm interested but there has to be more money."

I called Gloria, told her Roger was interested, but that we needed more money.

Gloria's response was: I've been thinking it over, David. Maybe I should use Bradshaw? Could you get him?"

"Yes," I answered.

"And Lynn Swann?"

"Sure, they're a team."

"Find out what they want. It has to be a package, both Bradshaw and Swann."

I called each player's agent. I felt the figures they were quoting were way out of line, but I accepted them because now I had some reference to negotiate for Staubach and Pearson.

I called Gloria and told her what Bradshaw and Swann wanted, and I added that while there was nothing wrong with Bradshaw and Swann, Roger Staubach was more the Xerox image—the clean-cut, All-American type.

"Okay," she said. "Will you accept what I offered the other day?"

"Gloria, you know that was a very low figure. I told you that. What Bradshaw and Swann are asking is more like it."

"How much for Staubach?" she asked.

"One hundred thousand."

"Too much, David, too much."

Before I could say anything else, she said, "We'll give him seventy-five."

"Okay," I said, keeping my voice level so as not to show my pleasure. I was looking at my notes. She had originally offered $30,000 and now we had settled on $75,000. I figured I could get the same increase for Pearson. "And for Drew Pearson?"

"Twenty-five."

"You have to be kidding. You gotta do better than that." I was adamant. I was also sure she'd raise it as she had with Roger.

But she fooled me. "Sorry, David. That's our budget—one hundred thousand for the package. Seventy-five for Roger, twenty-five for Drew."

I called Roger and told him he would get $75,000.

He was pleased. "And what about Drew?"

"That's a problem. They'll only give Drew twenty-five."

"No more?" he asked.

"No more."

He said, "Let me think about it overnight."

He called the next day. "David, I realize I wouldn't be the great quarterback I am without my teammate, Drew, making great catches. Here's what I want to do. Let's take all the money—mine and Drew's—put it on the table and split it in half."

I was surprised, but the more I thought about it, the more I was convinced Roger had that in mind from the very beginning.

The lesson? Simple: No man is an island.

For Super Bowl XVI, Detroit became the focal spot of the nation and hundreds of reporters were there looking for a story. Everybody wanted to meet Jack Reynolds and be the first to get the scoop on how he got the nickname Hacksaw. Jack didn't want to tell the story a zillion times, so he had Bill Walsh's secretary type up a press release. Whenever anyone approached Jack about the nickname, Jack took the photocopied sheets and handed one out.

Super Bowl week brings to one spot not only all the sports reporters in the country, but also all the representatives of sporting-goods manufacturers. Looking for player endorsements, they come in droves with bags and boxes and carloads of their equipment. Sneaker representatives, for example, are everywhere. You may have noticed that a lot of players wear Puma, Pony, Nike, and Adidas sneakers. They get paid to wear them to the Super Bowl, and the deals are concluded two or three days before the game for the majority of players. Other players have year-round deals.

I had heard a story that in 1981 a lot of the Rams were grabbing endorsements from every manufacturer and then, to comply with their contracts technically, ripped off the sides of their sneakers and pasted the labels on their feet. One player wore a Nike on one foot and a Puma on the other. Jack Youngblood was the uncontested winner of the game; he wound up with three different labels on one shoe and collected from all three companies.

In 1982 Jack Reynolds was bombarded with offers of thousands of dollars just to wear a particular make of sneaker for the game. I was supposed to go to Detroit early, but I couldn't get away until the last minute. So Jack kept telling the sneaker reps to call me in New York. I told them all I wanted was $5,000. No one was interested in paying that kind of money to one guy.

Bobby Hammond, a former Giants running back, was representing Pony. He said, "David, let Jack wear our sneakers in the Super Bowl."

"Fine." I replied and told him what I wanted.

"Too much, David. We'll go fifteen hundred."

"No deal."

Roger Vogel, the Puma rep, called and wanted Jack to wear his sneaks.

"Sure, he'd love to."

"We'll give him a thousand for wearing them and a bonus of five hundred if the Forty-niners win the game."

"Roger," I said, my voice somewhat disdainful, "we've already had other offers. We want five thousand, win or lose."

When I spoke with Jack, I asked him, "What do *you* want to wear?"

"Whichever I can make the most money on."

Then all of a sudden I got a call from Bobby Hammond. "I'll give you the deal at what you want." Just like that! "Let me get back to you," I said. "Jack has to make the decision."

I called Jack and discovered that he and Roger Vogel of Puma had been seeing a lot of each other in the last two days. "Roger told me I'm not in the bidding for Puma," Jack said. "So, we're just hanging out. We're getting to be good friends."

Now I understood what had happened. Bobby Hammond had seen Jack with the competition—Puma—and assumed Roger was getting close to Jack to get him to endorse their sneakers.

That evening I called Bobby back and told him that Jack

wanted $5,000 for wearing Pony sneakers during the Super Bowl. He agreed.

Later when I saw Bobby I asked him why he had paid so much. He told me he was certain the game was going to center around Jack. He convinced his boss, and he was right. Jack made the great goal-line stand wearing his Ponys, and everyone came out a winner.

Now, as for how good those sneakers were: Jack is known for calling huddles on the sidelines to go over defensive plays during the game. In the middle of the Super Bowl, in front of seventy million people, he called one of his famous sideline huddles while the 49ers had the ball. The guys came together and surrounded him, thinking he was going to diagram some play on the chalkboard. Instead, he unzipped his pants and moved around the circle of guys, peeing on everyone's sneakers.

One day I got a phone call from an agency doing a local TV commercial spot for Pioneer Chicken in California. Pioneer was giving away a Rams jacket as part of a charity-event promotion for their chicken. They wanted Vince Ferragamo, and we agreed on a price. A little later I was a bit hurt to find out Fred Dryer was also going to be in the commercial. After all, Fred had been using me as an agent.

I called Fred in California. "Why didn't you tell me?"

"A friend of mine asked me to do it, and I said I would."

I'm always suspicious of deals made through friends. "How much are they paying you?"

"A thousand dollars." Then as if to justify not getting me involved, Freddie added, "The same as Vince is getting."

"They told you Vince was getting a thousand?"

"No, they told me I was getting the same as Vince."

"Did you check with Vince?"

"No."

"Fred, you know me. Would I let Vince do a TV commercial for a thousand dollars?"

Silence on the other end of the phone.

"Next time, you call me before you agree to any commercial. That's what I'm here for!"

"But, David, this friend called, and I've known him for years."

"Terrific. Is that why he screwed you? He offered you a thousand because he's your friend?"

This is a common problem with a lot of celebrities. They meet an awful lot of people and become friendly with some who can—and do—get them business. Sometimes they're afraid that if an agent comes into the picture, they'll lose the deal. And of course the "friend" encourages the celebrity to think that way.

It was foolish for the ad agency to assume that Fred and Vince wouldn't talk. Promoters can easily lie to different entertainers and celebrities because they rarely meet at the same time. But football players aren't like nine-to-five employees in corporations, where people tend not to compare salaries because they don't want others to know what they are making. Athletes spend a lot of time together, and in football and other team sports, players hang around the locker room a lot, and they do talk and compare what they're getting for endorsements and appearances.

Vince and I showed up for the Pioneer Chicken commercial which was being shot on the football field at Long Beach State College, California. Vince and Fred were going to be with a young kid playing football, and would tell viewers how to get a free jacket with the purchase of some Pioneer Chicken. Vince was there, the kid was there, but no Fred Dryer. An hour went by, then two—still no Fred. The agency people didn't know what to do.

"I'll call him at home," I said finally. Sure enough, Fred was sitting there with a guy from Pioneer Chicken who had come to pick him up.

"David," Fred said. "You know why I'm not going to do that commercial? They said it was a favored-nations deal. But it isn't. I'm not getting the same as Vince is getting."

A "favored-nations" deal is a show business term used to indicate that the celebrities doing a series of commercials or guest-starring in a TV series, and doing essentially the same amount of work, will all earn the same amount of money. It is done as a favored-nations deal to eliminate any jealousy among the celebrities.

Well, this *wasn't* a favored-nations deal. What had happened was they had gone to Fred first because he was easy, and used a friend to make the contact. They offered him $1,000—and he accepted when they told him that's what they were going to offer Vince.

Then they called me but never told me Fred was going to do it. I made a totally separate agreement for Vince for a lot more money than they gave Fred. You have to be careful in these agreements. Just to be in a commercial and say, "Hi, I'm Vince Ferragamo," endorsing a product where the commercial will only run for thirteen weeks, is one thing. It's totally different if they want Vince to throw the football. A client has to get paid extra if he acts out what he does; that's his point of identity.

Now Fred said to me over the phone, "David, I feel I got screwed."

"What am I supposed to do now? It's too late. You made a deal with them yourself."

"Talk to them, David. I'll pay you."

"It's not the money. I really can't intercede." But then I thought, *Why not?* "Okay, Fred. I'm going to see what I can do."

I called up the owner of the ad agency and said, "If you want Fred Dryer in the commercial, I think it's only fair that you pay him the same as Vince."

"What!" he shouted at me. "You're holding me up!"

"No," I said calmly. "I'm acting as a go-between. This is what Fred told me to tell you. You made a deal with him."

"That's right." The guy was still belligerent. "A thousand dollars."

"You also told him it was a 'favored-nations' deal; he was getting the same money as Vince Ferragamo."

"Huh . . .?" His voice had lost all its anger. "I'll call you right back."

A half-hour later he called back. "Fred can have the same money as Vince."

CHAPTER

10

THE FIGHT GAME

Many times I see a client's present negotiating position and his future somewhat differently from the way the client sees them. Nevertheless, I believe it is my duty to steer him to what I regard as the best possible road to take. Sometimes, unfortunately, a client is his own worst enemy, and all my plans and efforts go down the drain, as I found out when I first got into the fight game.

I was up at Grossinger's to accept an award being presented to Lou Piniella from the Yonkers Safari, a philanthropic organization of professional men who plan a week up in Grossinger's once a year. It's a getaway for these men, a chance to meet athletes, and at the same time it's an opportunity to raise some money for charity.

One of the guests was Don King, the boxing promoter. Don's background is known to most people in the fight game. In the sixties, he spent four and a half years in prison on a manslaughter rap. (Recently the governor of Ohio granted him a full pardon.) He's a big man, six feet three inches and over 225 pounds. King is the right name for him—his hair looks like a crown, always standing straight up as if full of static.

Don has made himself the king of fight promotion. As soon as he got out of prison in 1968, he managed Earnie Shavers, who was then using Archie Moore, the great light heavyweight champion, as his trainer. That was Don's start, and now at Grossinger's he was getting a well-deserved award for his contributions to the sport. Don was one of those who pushed boxing onto television, closed-circuit TV, cable. He saw the potential of markets other than boxing arenas. He took boxing from a nickel-and-dime business and turned it into a million-dollar one.

If there was ever a hotel that had a Jewish image, it's Grossinger's, in the heart of the Catskills. And Don King knew where he was. He got up and delivered a ten-minute speech in Yiddish. The place was roaring. Those who understood Yiddish were laughing their sides off, and those who didn't understand were impressed and were swept along with the laughter around them.

That was my introduction to boxing, watching and listening to Don King up in Grossinger's. I knew I was watching a real promoter. I shouldn't have been surprised that it happened at Grossinger's rather than at Madison Square Garden or at Gleason's Gym, because boxing has been a part of the hotel since the thirties. In those days, Milton Blackstone, who did marketing work for Grossinger's, suggested Barney Ross train up there. "Who needs the stinking, sweaty gym?" Blackstone told Ross. "Go to the mountains. Fresh air. Good food. Nice people."

Grossinger's built a training gym and soon realized it had a wonderful promotion vehicle. Celebrities followed Ross to the mountains. The press came to see him train and report on his condition. Soon there were datelines from Grossinger's about champions and contenders alike: Rocky Marciano, Dick Tiger, Nino Benvenuti, Joey Archer, Ken Norton, Larry Holmes, Roberto Duran, Ray (Boom-Boom) Mancini, and Michael Spinks, to name a few.

I was up there one weekend in February 1981, watching Trevor Berbick train for his fight against the World Heavyweight champion, Larry Holmes. I was sitting at ringside as Berbick's sparring and started feeling the excitement of the sport. It's brutal force "civilized," raw animal power, tempered with skill and style. I loved it, and I wanted to get involved.

I was sitting with Mark Etess, vice-president and general manager of Grossinger's, whom I've known for years. He's smart and as sharp as a tack, one of the youngest GM's of a major hotel in the country. He is not much older than I; at that time he was twenty-nine, I was twenty-four.

With the adrenaline pumping through my blood, I turned to Mark. "I've never been turned on like this before. You have all these great athletes up here. Why don't you and I go into representing some professional boxers?"

Mark looked at me. There was a slight smile, no, a smirk, at the corners of his mouth. As GM at Grossinger's, he hears a hundred crazy schemes a day. "Hey," he said. "What do I need it for? I'm already running a hotel in my spare time."

"Mark." I leaned over. "You know these guys. You've been up here since you were a kid." (Mark is Jenny Grossinger's grandson. There's a picture in his office showing him being held by Rocky Marciano, who was the heavyweight champ when Mark was four years old.) "You know the fight game. I know promotion."

Now I was thinking about all the fights I had seen on TV or read about. There is always a hubbub, an entourage, a bunch of celebrities around boxers. Why? What was turning me on turned them on—strength, power, skill, competition, but not as a team sport. This is done toe to toe, man to man. Probably every man's fantasy is to be able to fight as well as the guy they're watching in the ring. It's projection, sublimation, voyeurism, and it's worth a fortune!

I looked back at the ring. The fighters were grunting as they pounded each other. Sweat came flying off their bodies with each hit. "What about Berbick? Does he have a manager?"

Trevor Berbick, a Jamaican, was then the Canadian heavyweight champion, but in those days he wasn't as well known, as he is now. Then he was just someone halfway down the ratings who got a shot at Holmes because he'd surprised everyone by beating John Tate in the preliminary fight before the Sugar Ray Leonard-Duran fight in Montreal.

"I don't know too much about his arrangement," Mark told me. "I got a call from Murray Goodman, Don King's publicity man, asking me to house him here while he trains. He's staying at the house next to mine, so we see a lot of each other. He's a nice, soft-spoken man. Very pleasant."

I almost shouted: "Does he have a manager?"

"There's Don Kerr, but I don't think he's been with Trevor too long."

"Find out, and let's do something."

Nothing happened. Mark had a lot of other things to contend with, and I was running around the country for my clients.

In April Trevor Berbick went into the ring with Larry Holmes and went the distance—a full fifteen rounds with the champion. At that time he was the only man to have done that. He lost.

I called Mark. "What's with Berbick? Can we sign him? He's good. He's got something. He needs someone to take care of his business." I was ready to go out and promote him. My enthusiasm excited Mark and he made a couple of calls to track Berbick down.

He finally reached him up in Nova Scotia. "How are you, Trevor?"

"Feeling good, mon. Just sorry I lost the fight."

"You fought well."

"I 'urt my thumb in the first round."

"Sure," Mark said, somewhat cynically.

"No, no," Trevor insisted. "It's true."

Mark had watched the fight and put it on tape, so after the call, he replayed it. Surprisingly, the camera had followed Trevor back to his corner after the first round. There was Trevor pointing to his thumb, and you could read his lips as he was telling his trainer, "I 'urt my thumb."

"You did terrific with Holmes, though," Mark said to him.

"Yeah. I could 'ave beat him. I went the distance." Mark heard the pride in Trevor's voice. "It got me another good fight."

"Oh? Who is it?"

"Promise you won't tell anyone until it's announced."

"Sure. I won't say a word."

"Someone's trying to set up a fight between me and Muhammad Ali."

"Who?" Mark was surprised, although he shouldn't have been. Ali was out there looking for someone to fight for a big purse. Trevor coming off the Holmes fight would be a perfect draw . . . if anyone was still interested in watching Ali shuffle around the ring.

It was a fight that no one in the United States wanted to touch. A company, Sports International, was formed to promote the fight in the Bahamas. Eventually it was staged in a converted sandlot-baseball field. Trevor went into it without a manager. "I'm taking care of the details," he told Mark over the phone. Mark and Berbick were talking once a week now and becoming good friends. Mark kept telling him he should have someone go over the contract, thinking of me. But Berbick was sure he could do it all himself.

Weeks before the fight, the first signs of confusion began to show. The promoters hadn't made any arrangements for Trevor to stay in the Bahamas. Mark called a friend of his at the Bahamas Princess Hotel in Freeport and got some rooms for Trevor and his crew.

Trevor called to thank Mark. Again Mark tried to get him to have someone go over the contract. "No, mon. Nothing to worry about. You gotta come to the fight. I'll send tickets." The tickets arrived and Mark went to the Bahamas with his wife, Lauren.

The day before the fight there had been a whole to-do. Trevor publicly stated that he hadn't received any money, and there would be no fight until he got paid.

Mark went to see Trevor in his hotel room the afternoon of the fight. He was hardly in the door when the fighter started complaining. "No money, mon. They ain't given me any money." The promoters were full of surprises—no money, only surprises. Here it was 4:45, the day of the fight, and all Trevor had was a worthless contract. He was insisting on cash or a valid letter of credit.

James Cornelius, the original promoter, seemed to have disappeared. At five o'clock, Mark was there with Trevor and his trainer, Lee Black, when a man came to the suite holding an attaché case. He didn't introduce himself. He wanted to talk to Trevor, alone.

Trevor took the man into the bedroom. Twenty minutes later they came out. The man was still holding his attaché case, and Trevor was all smiles. "Fight's on." He winked at Mark and held out several thousand-dollar ringside seats, like a kid handing out candy. Trevor thought he had something, but there was no one down there who would pay $1,000 a seat. Mark didn't know how much money the guy gave him—if anything—but whatever was said and done in that bedroom satisfied Trevor, and the fight was on.

Except suddenly they realized there were no gloves and no bell for the ring. It is the promoter's responsibility to supply gloves for the entire card. At 5:30 they had to hire a private plane to go to Miami and get boxing gloves. Mind you, the first fight was on at 8:00 P.M.

They never did get a bell for the ring; they wound up using an old cow bell. Trevor, of course, beat Ali in a decision, and I was on the phone with Mark as soon as he got back to New York. "What are we going to do with Berbick?" I asked him.

"He wants to handle everything himself," Mark said. "I'm certain he's getting screwed, but there's nothing I can do."

"He's crazy. He should concentrate on boxing. He's in the public eye now. I can get him all kinds of deals."

"I'll talk to him," Mark said. Next thing I heard was that Mark wrote Trevor a long letter. Mark told Trevor he was amazed how he could go into the ring and beat Ali under the circumstances. Mark went on to explain that all the contractual commitments should have been handled by competent people, and it should have been done long before the day of the fight. Money was the last thing Berbick should have to worry about before getting into the ring because the minute he got into the ring, he would have no leverage. It all had to be signed, settled, and delivered long before the fight.

Trevor wasn't interested. He appreciated Mark's concern, but still thought he could do it all himself. Okay, you couldn't force him to do it. It was his life, but he was missing a golden opportunity.

And who got the preliminary fight for the highly touted Cooney-Holmes card? Berbick! Watching the fight, I couldn't believe how good he was. Even though he had gone the distance with Holmes and beaten Ali, he came into the ring against Greg Page as an underdog. It made sense, however, because he had had no promotion. Berbick beat Page decisively, and I was on the phone to Mark.

"David," Mark said, "I've talked to Trevor until I'm blue in the face. You call and talk to him. He'll be back up in Nova Scotia in a few days. I'll tell him you're going to call."

I did. I was on the phone with Berbick three and a half hours, talking about boxing, about promotion, about endorsements. We talked about Mark and me managing him. "Mon," he said, "I want you to represent me. Be my agent. Go ahead and send me the papers."

As soon as I got off the phone, I called shoe companies, boxing-equipment manufacturers to sound people out for endorsements. They were interested, but they all wanted to know when his next fight would be and against whom.

I called Berbick. "We have to set up a fight. It's important we do it soon. Some people are thinking of using you, and we have to show them you're going to be staying in the public eye."

"Can't talk now," he said. "I'm on my way to Miami. I'll give you a call when everything's settled there."

A warning bell was going off in my head. "Settled there? What's happening?"

"I'll talk to you, I'll talk to you." And that was it.

A week later, Berbick called. "Mon, you gotta come down to Miami tomorrow."

"*Tomorrow?*"

"We're 'aving a press conference. Don King is coming down to set up a fight for me with Scott Franks. I want you there."

Now he's talking, I thought; we were in business. I called Mark. "Listen, you have to come to New York, now." It was six in the evening. "We're on the nine-thirty from Newark."

"Hold it," Mark replied. "What's going on?"

I told him about Berbick's call. He was probably holding the phone at arm's length, I was talking so fast and so loud. I looked at my watch. Mark was up in the Catskills, and it would take him two hours to get to Newark. I was halfway through telling him what Berbick said when he interrupted me: "Stop, I'm packing my bag. See you at Newark."

I met Mark at nine o'clock; we were on our way to Miami, smiling and happy. We were getting into the fight game, as managers, agents of the *next heavyweight champion of the world*. We could hear it being announced from the ring at Madison Square Garden. At least, that's what we were telling ourselves.

Sometimes you get a clue to the kind of day you're going to have. Little things happen that you shrug off but, when seen in retrospect, are warnings.

Well, our flight was late, and we didn't get to our motel, the Golden Blades Holiday Inn where Berbick was staying, until 2:30 A.M. Miami was sweltering. It was July, but our room wasn't air-conditioned. At first, they didn't want to change our room; instead, a mechanic came to fix the air conditioner. All he did was make a lot of noise, and by the time we got another room and went to sleep, it was almost four o'clock.

At eight we met Berbick for breakfast. This was the first time I had actually met him, but we felt we knew each other because we had been talking so much over the telephone.

"This is going to be great," he said, looking at Mark and me. "Don King is coming down, and I want you two to be involved."

We couldn't ask him about our arrangements because he was with Hank Kaplan, a sports publicity man for the Miami area who arranged the press conference. The city of Miami had converted Tropical Park racetrack into a municipal park with a boxing center. Kaplan told us that Trevor was going to move to Miami and use Tropical Park as his training center, and the press conference was to publicize it.

Mark and I looked at each other, then at Berbick.

"Don's coming down," he said to us. "I'm moving to Miami. I like to train in tropical climates. I want to introduce you guys to the press. I'll introduce you to the media and everything. It's at the Omni."

Berbick and Kaplan drove to the Omni in one car, Mark and I in another, but we couldn't find a press conference. No one was there. It turned out the conference was being held next door to the Omni, at a Chinese restaurant owned by a friend of Angelo Dundee's. That should have told us something about our relationship with Berbick, but we weren't reading the signs.

We came in while the press conference was going on. It was packed with reporters and TV people. Berbick was good, cracking jokes, talking about Miami and Tropical Park, saying all the right things.

Listening to the way he handled himself with the media, I realized that with his record, all he needed was promotion. A lot of the business—with any celebrity—is PR. I was thinking I would do for him what Dennis Rappaport and Mike Jones (Cooney's managers) did for him; they made him over ten million dollars—basically on promotion.

With the right kind of exposure and publicity, Berbick could be right up there. He hadn't promoted himself. Even with his record, he was still unknown. He hadn't tried to exploit his fight with Holmes or his defeat of Ali. He should have used the Ali fight as a springboard to fame. Instead, he won and went home. Mark and I had decided to build a reputation for Trevor in New York. We were going to get him a fight at the Garden and sell it to Home Box Office—just for New York, with world rights going out afterward. We would build a base of support for him and then spread it out. Trevor was still young enough for two years of careful matchmaking. By thirty he would be champ.

"Who's your next fight?" a reporter asked Berbick.

We hadn't been able to talk to Trevor alone, hadn't been able to tell him what we planned. We waved our hands in the air, shook our heads from side to side, hoping Trevor would see us, understand what we meant, and say nothing.

Trevor looked around the room. "Don King is supposed to come down here. He'll tell you."

I turned to Mark, who was already staring at me. "What the hell are we doing here?"

"Don will soon be here," Berbick went on. "But first I want you to meet my new agents." He introduced us to the media.

After the press conference, I went over to Berbick. "Trevor, what's this about Don King?"

"Don called this morning at the motel. He left a message he couldn't make it. But Duke Durden's down. He'll meet us at the gym."

At the gym at Tropical Park, we met Duke Durden, an ex-football player and a former Nevada athletic commissioner, and another guy, Pedro. Don't ask who Pedro was; it's *what* he was. Big! Six feet three inches, maybe six feet four, huge shoulders, a huge stomach. And he had an interesting set of rings—enormous ones on each finger—and he kept his fingers close together so

there was no mistaking what the rings were for. That was Pedro—
just the kind of guy you want to do business with.

Trevor went into the dressing room after working out, and I
followed him in, wanting to know what was going on. Duke followed me. Mark—who had been around the fight business a long
time and didn't need it spelled out for him—stayed outside with
Hank Kaplan and Pedro.

Berbick started telling Duke who I was. Duke said nothing; he
didn't even look at me. He went over to Berbick and said, "You
don't need an agent. You and me will sit down and we'll do the
fight."

"I want David involved," said Berbick.

Duke had handed Berbick a contract. Trevor got $75,000 for
fighting Holmes. He thought Don King needed him, so he took
the $75,000 and hoped Don would appreciate it. Between the
gate and TV, the fight netted a couple of million dollars, and
Trevor Berbick got $75,000. Some businessman!

Now Duke was telling him who he was going to fight. "It's in
the contract," he said. "Scott Franks and Renaldo Snipes. You
signed for a series of fights for Don."

Berbick walked over to me and handed me the contract.

Duke's voice boomed out from the other side of the room: "You
don't need an agent. You and me can do business. We'll take care
of you."

Berbick turned to Duke. "I want David to sit in."

"I don't think Don will like that."

Berbick tugged at my arm and started leading me to the door.
"Listen, I won't sign anything, I promise. Just let me do the talking. You go look over the contract. I'll meet you at the coffee shop
in the motel."

I sat in a booth in the coffee shop and read through the contract. At the bottom of one page it said the promoter had the right
to promote the next three fights. When Trevor slid into the
booth, I asked him about it.

"I never agreed to anything but the one fight with Holmes."

I showed him the clause.

"I never saw it."

"Did you *read* it?" I asked him.

He looked at me. "Sure I read it!" But something told me he hadn't, or maybe it had been left blank and filled in afterward, you never know. "Well, it's here. You have no choice. You have to fight whoever Don King says you're going to fight."

Now Berbick was angry. "No, mon, no, mon. I don't 'ave to do it." He banged his fist down on the table.

While we were talking, Duke and Pedro came into the coffee shop, and they pushed themselves onto the seats next to us— Duke next to Berbick, Pedro next to me. I'm big, but Pedro was bigger and he kept pushing me into the wall. He knew exactly what he was doing.

"Trevor," said Duke, totally ignoring me, "I need you to sign this contract."

"I want a hundred thousand dollars for one fight."

"That's not enough," I said. Suddenly I felt Pedro pushing me further toward the wall.

"Look, Trevor," Duke said, "I'll be honest with you. I need you to sign. Don needs you to sign so we can go to ABC."

I understood what they were doing. They would take the contract to ABC-TV and say, "Berbick has agreed to fight Franks and Snipes," and they would get a commitment and up-front money from ABC for exclusive coverage. It's the same in the movie business. If you get Robert Redford to agree to a script, you can sell it to a studio and get your money to make it.

But they were talking two fights on television and $100,000 a fight was peanuts. "Why don't you leave the money clause blank?" I said, thinking that once the fights were announced, Berbick could sit down with some leverage and negotiate with Don King. "Let's make a notation that the amount will be negotiated later."

Duke looked at me. "Yeah. Let's do that." Duke was probably agreeing because he was used to contracts with blank spaces.

I got a flight back to New York that night, thinking I was finally beginning to get this together. I expected to hear from Don King to work out the terms of the contract.

Instead, I got a call from Berbick. "Don King called. He wants me to fight Snipes in mid-August for national television. He wants it in Cleveland."

"Have you agreed to anything?" I asked.

"No, mon. Maybe I'll fight, maybe I won't."

King convinced Berbick to fight Snipes in Cleveland with a promise that the winner would meet Holmes.

Two weeks before the fight, Berbick called. "I can't fight. I don't feel well." I was happy to hear it. Maybe he finally understood what was happening. He was ranked higher than Snipes and had nothing to win by fighting. King ordered Berbick to Cleveland to have his own doctor examine him. The doctor agreed with Berbick's doctor in Miami—he could not fight.

Don King didn't say a word to anyone. He had already sold the fight to ABC's *Wide World of Sports*. In fact, the only purpose of the fight was to sell it to TV. Days went by, but still no word came that Berbick couldn't fight.

I called Bob Iger at ABC and told him about Berbick.

"What?" he said, surprised. "We've got it all lined up. We haven't heard a word about Berbick being sick."

"I'm telling you. There's not going to be a fight."

What eventually happened was that Don King flew into New York two days before the scheduled fight and tried to sell ABC two other boxers for the same amount of money. ABC said no and canceled the fight. But the competition to get boxing on the air was so strong, CBS picked it up immediately and carried it.

Berbick called me a week later after he had spoken to Don King. "Don wants me to fight Snipes in October."

"Trevor"—I was trying to figure out how to get through to him—"you have one job, to fight. You should begin training. Just think about boxing. Let me handle the business. Don't do any more talking."

"But what if Don calls?"

"Tell him to call me. I'll take care of it for you."

I placed a couple of calls to King, but he didn't return them. Instead, Berbick phoned me a few days later. "Don's set a fight in Atlantic City."

"What?" I sank down in my chair. It was crazy. He didn't listen. Yet I felt I had to go through it all with him again. "I thought I was going to handle this."

"You are, David."

"What do you mean I am? You're telling me you settled with Don!"

"Just for this one fight in Atlantic City."

"Who?"

"Snipes."

"You're crazy. Didn't Mark talk to you about this before? You have nothing to win by fighting Snipes."

"Don asked me to do him a favor."

"I see. How much is he paying you for this favor?"

"Well . . . we 'aven't talked exact money. He says he'll take care of me."

"He says he'll take care of you?" I was thinking of what Mark had told me about the Bahamas. It was happening to Berbick again. "Why did you do it?"

Trevor's voice was full of confidence. "Don't worry, David, I know what I'm doing. You don't 'ave to get involved. I'm handling everything."

"Ah ha. Yes, you are." I knew it was time for me to back off. There was nothing to be gained here.

"Look," Trevor went on, "after this one, I get to fight Larry Holmes."

"Larry Holmes? You have that in the contract?"

"I don't need it in the contract. Don gave me his word. I trust Don King." He paused a while—perhaps he was thinking—and then added, "If he doesn't do it, I'll beat him up."

Great philosophy! "What about the money for this fight?"

"Don says he'll take care of me after the fight."

Why go on? It was hopeless. There was no way to get through to Berbick. He was in the unfortunate position of knowing a little, and confusing what he knew and what he didn't know. He was an expert at boxing; so—he should box. Instead, he was trying to be an expert on the business side, too.

"Trevor," I said, "I wish you the best of luck. I hope you win. I hope you get your money."

And that was the end of it—or so I thought. The day before the fight, I got a call. "David. It's me, Trevor."

"Hey, how are you?"

"Great, mon. The fight's tomorrow. I've got your tickets. I need you, mon. Come down."

I was impressed he was asking me to come watch him, to sit in his corner. "Sure, I'll come down."

"Great, mon! And will you do me a favor?"

Suddenly I realized he had something else in mind. "What's that?"

"I need a cup for my groin."

"A protector?" I couldn't believe it. The day before the fight, and he still didn't have all his equipment.

I went to Atlantic City with the protector, and it was the Bahamas revisited. He had no contract, and no money. Two hours before the fight, Berbick stormed into Duke's office demanding $300,000.

"What?" Duke asked, looking up at Berbick.

"Three hundred thousand dollars, or I don't fight."

"Okay, don't fight. We'll give ABC back the money. You can go home and stay there forever!"

Berbick was standing with nowhere to go. "Okay, I'll fight."

Berbick got in the ring, but he *didn't* fight. From the first round you could tell he had no concentration. Snipes got in a couple of good shots and knocked Berbick down in the first round. Trevor got up, but he'd lost the fight before he even got into the ring because he was worrying about everything except boxing. Certainly, he was thinking about his money. He wanted to do it his way—and he did.

There is a great lesson to be learned here because this story illustrates all the reasons why people fail to get what they deserve.

To put it most simply, you must know what you want. Not just for today, but down the line. And then everything you do must become part of that picture you have in mind. You must also know your skills, what you're good at and what limitations you have.

If you are in a position to afford an agent—a negotiator—use his skills to complement what you can do. Let him get you what he can while you concentrate on what you are good at. If you can't afford someone to take up the slack, then define what *you* can do.

Set a realistic goal. Aim for something you can accomplish and go after it. In the process of achieving that goal you will be learning all the time. Learn the rules, go out and negotiate for yourself; begin to use the techniques, a little at a time, until you become more and more confident. Once you reach your goal, redefine it! Set your sights higher.

11

TRICKS OF THE TRADE

T he best advice I can leave with you are some "tricks of the trade." But they are not really tricks, but sound negotiating techniques that you can use yourself to go out and get what you deserve in life.

Attitude

You have to walk into any negotiation with a positive attitude. If you come in with anything less, you're going to get beat. It's all in the confidence you have when you walk in, a feeling that everyone in the room is good, but that *you* are the best.

How do you gain confidence? By knowing why you're there and what you're doing. A lot of people try to memorize everything and go over it in their minds a hundred times. The worst feeling in the world is to leave a negotiation thinking, "I should have said such and such." *Don't rely on your memory.* Write things down; come prepared with a written agenda you want to cover. In my meetings with George Steinbrenner, I must have had a hundred and fifty points ready to shoot back at the man. If you want to win, you have to have ammunition. You can have all the confidence in the world, but if you come unprepared and don't know what you're talking about, you're going to come out a loser.

Suppose you walk into your boss's office for a raise and he says, "We didn't have such a good year," what do you do? You have to expect something like that. Make sure you know the answer *be-*

fore you see him face-to-face. Get hold of the records, check out the annual report. If you can, get your personnel record with your boss's comments written on it. Keep your own personal record, how you are doing. But don't just say, "I think we're doing great." Walk in with *specifics*.

A lady who worked in a boutique was taking my negotiations course. She was complaining that she was earning $250 a week instead of $350 or $400. I asked her why she thought she deserved so much more.

"Because I'm a great saleslady. I turn over a lot of business and the old customers keep coming back to me. *They ask for me by name.*"

I told her to keep a record of her sales. She did. In one week she found that she had made sales totaling $7,000. If you took off 50 percent of the cost of the goods and then deducted more for overhead, etc., the net she was making for the boutique came to $2,500 a week. Now she had some ammunition for face-to-face negotiations.

When she confronted her employer, he was amazed, and he couldn't argue with the facts because she presented them very carefully. She walked out with a raise boosting her pay to $425 a week.

Body Language

How you sit, how you look, how you move around during the negotiations are all very important. Stride into a room. Shake hands forcefully. Look your opponent in the eye, let him or her know you're there on business. If you're sitting on the edge of your chair, nervous and tense, it's different from sitting back, legs crossed in a relaxed, unconcerned manner. I always go into negotiations with the attitude that I don't have to be there. *This doesn't mean I don't have to be there.* Obviously I'm there because I want to be, and, in many cases, I need to be there. But I *assume* an attitude to calm me down.

You've got to keep telling yourself: "I've got money in the bank; I don't have to be here. I don't need the other side." One of the reasons I stress having a second job is that it gives you the confidence to adopt this attitude.

Opening Ploys

You must talk up. You can tell lack of purpose when someone starts sentences with "Ah . . . eh . . . uh." Never use these grunts. Many times when you begin negotiations, the tension is very high. Try to start out on a personal note; perhaps a short story that will appeal to the other side's interest, or some item *other* than what you are negotiating for.

I had several tough negotiations with George Young of the New York Giants over several lunches, but each lunch meeting started off on a personal note. George gave me a "some of my best friends are Jewish" routine. He told me he had taught at a Jewish camp. He told me he used to be a schoolteacher, knowing my mother was a schoolteacher. I wasn't offended. I enjoyed it. He had done some homework on me, and I credit him with that.

Through John Shaw, vice-president of finance for the Los Angeles Rams, I found out George Young's nickname is "Sweats." All the GM's call him that. We started talking about how he got his name. Don McCalley, the former running back of the Colts, told the story that when George used to give a team meeting, there was always a puddle of sweat on the floor around him. All that chitchat eased the way to the negotiations. We developed rapport, and *then* we were able to go into bargaining.

Bluffing

It's tough when you have to bluff. If you don't have anything behind you, you really shouldn't do it. My advice on bluffing is very easy: Take a pencil and paper and write down what can happen if the deal goes through, and what happens to you and to the other side if it doesn't. It's as simple as that.

Try to have all the facts of your situation, and then have an alternative if the bluff fails. Before you threaten to quit, go out and see if you *can* get another job. Find out what your worth is to your company.

It's very easy to bluff when you negotiate a free-agent contract in baseball because you can go out and make a deal with another team and come in to negotiate a shot for the moon.

Ron Jackson had an agent who accepted a Detroit Tigers offer for three quarters of a million dollars for three years. There were no other offers on the table. After Jallil accepted the Detroit offer, he turned around and demanded more money. He felt that since Detroit agreed to three quarters of a million, they would go a little higher. He said there were others interested. Jim Campbell, the Detroit general manager, took back his offer. Ron was left with nothing. Jallil had bluffed and failed because there was nothing behind him.

Spring training was on and Ron didn't have a job. I met him right before the 1982 season. We were both having breakfast—at different tables—at the Jolly Roger in Anaheim. Mario Dalessi, the Jolly Roger's general manager, introduced us, and Ron told me what had happened. He also said the Angels were showing some interest in him, but wanted to send him down to the minor leagues because he had missed spring training. Ron asked me if there was anything I could do for him. I said I would try.

I called Buzzie Bavasi, and we worked out a one-year deal. A one-year contract is not as bad as it sounds, because under major-league rules the player can declare free agency after the season ends.

Halfway through the season, I called Buzzie, and he invited me to sit with him and Gene Autry during the game. When the game was over, I asked Bavasi about signing Ron to a new contract, since Ron was playing extremely well behind Rod Carew and was coming off the bench and producing.

"We'll talk at the end of the season" was all Buzzie said.

After the season, I called Bavasi. He didn't return my calls. Instead, he had his assistant, Mike Port, call me. Buzzie was training Port to negotiate contracts for the Angels.

That was all right with me; everyone has to learn. I was only interested in getting Ron a good contract. If Mike Port could do it for me, fine. "Are you interested in meeting me prior to the free-agent draft?" I asked Mike.

"I'll get back to you."

When he called back, he said, "No. We'll talk after the free-agent draft." He also recommended Ron file for free agency.

Ron filed two weeks before the draft. As soon as Ron's name went over the wire, I got a call from Buzzie, huffing and puffing. "How dare you allow Ron to file for free agency!"

"Buzzie," I said, "I called you last week. The message I got from Port was you didn't want Ron."

"What do you want?" Buzzie asked.

"I want a three-year guarantee at one point two million dollars."

"No way. I can't afford it."

"That's what we want," I reiterated.

"Let me get back to you," Buzzie said.

Mike Port called back. His offer was for $800,000. I couldn't accept it.

Ron was playing baseball in Venezuela at that time. Before he left, he had sent me an autographed photo with the inscription: "Now it's my turn to get the big one." By the big one, he meant over a million.

I realized, of course, that Buzzie wanted Ron. He was using Port as a buffer in hopes of getting Ron for less than I was asking. Instead of calling Port back, I called Bavasi. He still couldn't offer Ron the $1.2 million. I started listing the salaries of comparable ballplayers. Prior to the recent football players' strike, the Major League Baseball Players Association, led by Marvin Miller and Peter Rose, had a totally different attitude about agents from that of the National Football League Players Association. The baseball association gave agents salary information so the agents had factual material when they entered negotiations. They don't feel they are in an adversary position with players' agents. So I had facts to deal with.

The three-way negotiations went on—with me calling Buzzie and he getting back to me through Mike Port. We came down to the wire right before the free-agent draft. Port called me and offered $1.1 million. I called Buzzie. "Why can't we have one point two million dollars?"

"No."

"Let's split the difference," I suggested.

"David, how can I go behind Mike Port's back? His final offer is one point one."

"What?" I laughed. "You've been going behind Port's back for a week and a half."

"Okay. I'll have Mike call you back."

He did, and we settled for $1.1 million guaranteed.

Don't bluff unless you've done your homework. I bluffed only because I had other teams showing interest; so I had somewhere to go if the bluff didn't work out. Bluffing is a calculated risk; be sure you're prepared.

Rejecting

Most agents and negotiators like to show the other side *their* power by saying, "I can make the deal." Paul Caruso showed the Rams how powerful he was by saying he guaranteed Vince's decision; he could control him himself. Well, you saw what happened.

Most agents take it upon themselves to be the big, strong up-front man. I don't believe that's an agent's job. My job is to negotiate for the client to make sure he gets *fair value*, that he gets what he wants, what he deserves. As an agent it's important for me to advise my clients only, not to make the final decision. So if a person on the other side of the table says, "Let's close the deal," I can say, "Listen, I can't make a commitment to you. I have to go back to my client."

That's why it's important for a negotiator to go in by himself and not with the client. Too many unskilled—or inexperienced— people show their reaction to an offer immediately. That's giving away too much information to the other side.

If a deal is bad, never say, "The hell with you. I'm leaving!" Always try to leave the door open. There are many ways to reject an offer—"I don't really like the deal," "I feel I deserve more," "I'd like to think it over." I always say, "Let me take the offer to my client and find out what he thinks." If I feel it's a good deal, then I tell the other side I'm going to recommend that my client take it.

Playing Smartass

Don't! Respect the person you're negotiating with. If someone is negotiating with you, you want something from him. Trying to outsmart the other side is not the way to do it. Outfoxing your opponent may give you a moment's ego trip, but you'll never get what you want from the meeting.

You always have to think of the other side. *Why* is the boss telling you you shouldn't get a raise? Let's say the man who heads the salary negotiations has a budget of $1,000,000 and he's given a $10.00 bonus for every thousand below the million. He's out there trying to make a living, *just like you.* You know he's not going to want to give you a raise, so you can't go into the meeting being a smartass.

Wishful Thinking

There is no sense saying "I want this, I deserve that" without coming in with ammunition that proves what you *want* is what you *deserve.* Just putting in your time doesn't give you a right to demand. Contributing to success—whether in profit or prestige—does give you the right to a piece of it.

There are many agents who say, "Every other quarterback is making so much, and therefore I want the same for my client." I don't buy that. Sure, I look at what other players are making, but I also look at my player's statistics. What has he done to contribute to a team's victories?

The best clients for whom to negotiate are winners whose personal contributions are greater than the statistics they compile. It's what they bring to the team in motivation—the winning attitude. People like Jack Reynolds and Lou Piniella have tremendous influence on their teammates and help make the team a winner. That's an invaluable asset.

Attacking Others

There is a right way and a wrong way to do this. Insulting someone is the wrong way. Proving someone wrong by pointing out the *facts* is an excellent way. You will always be helped in negotiations by showing you know what's going on, as long as you do it without acting superior. Having a little more information, a little more knowledge than the other side, puts you miles ahead. But don't use the information as blackmail; that's no good either. Have your facts up front and use them when the time comes.

Screaming and yelling is a dumb way to negotiate, yet thousands of people do bargain this way. That's what killed the 1982 football negotiations—each side going to reporters and putting the other down.

Why insult people? All it does is show how weak *your* position is. Remember, my motto is "Kill them with kindness." That's been my trick to make the other side feel important. In most cases, they will reciprocate and try to make *you* feel important—often by giving you what you're asking for.

Check the Facts

During negotiations people present a lot of "facts" of their own. Don't take them at face value. When I first started talking to Don Klosterman about Vince, Klosterman kept telling me, "This is what I gave Johnny Unitas." About three weeks into the negotiations I was booking entertainment into Caesar's Palace in Atlantic City when I found out Unitas was doing a radio show there. I approached him, introduced myself, told him I represented Vince Ferragamo, and asked him about his negotiations with Klosterman.

"Klosterman?" Johnny said. "I never dealt with Don Klosterman. I always negotiated with the owner, Carroll Rosenbloom."

So, check the facts.

Learn to Listen

You must learn to listen—not only to what is being said, but to what is left unsaid.

I was negotiating a contract for a free agent. The deadline was Saturday night for the original team to make a deal. I had had several offers through the week. I had spoken with my client. We were going to accept the last deal they gave us on Friday afternoon. I say Friday afternoon because I do not answer my phones on the Jewish Sabbath.

Somehow, we never got together on Friday. All day Saturday my phones were ringing, but I did not answer them. It made me think. Who was calling? Was it the team? Were they so interested that they continued to call? Late Saturday night, after the sun went down and the Sabbath was over, I answered the first phone call. Sure enough, it was the general manager. The first words out of his mouth were, "David, we've been trying to get you all day."

"Why?"

"We'll give you the extra one hundred thousand. We're going to accept your deal."

Revenge

Most people think of revenge as negative—that it means to get *back* at someone else. If you got into a negotiation seeking vengeance, that's all you'll get. You may get even, but what will it leave you with? Will *you* be better off?

Many times the desire for revenge can stand in the way of getting what you deserve. That's why in negotiations of a very personal nature, it's always best to use an agent, a lawyer, even a friend who can remain unemotional and objective.

But revenge also has its positive side, it's a question of channeling the energy. One of the reasons Jack Reynolds wanted to play in San Francisco was because the 49ers were playing the Rams twice that season. When he walked into the stadium, he was revved up to do damage, and in so doing he motivated a lot of his teammates.

Use revenge positively—to better yourself. If you want to get back at your boss, what will a work slowdown *give* you? Use that same energy to do *so* much better that eventually he'll have no choice but to move you up or lose you.

Perks and Bonuses

There are many ways of getting rewarded other than through a straight salary: an interest-free loan, an automobile, vacations, a bonus based on your performance, etc.

I was able to get Jack Reynolds a clause in his contract stating that he gets a bonus if he leads his team in tackles, and another bonus for each game they win. He also got a fully furnished apartment in San Francisco. These are all motivational factors for him. He is so aware of the bonuses that he keeps his own records. And for him, each game means not only winning but working toward that extra money.

Perks are a very good incentive for workers. If an employee does over a certain amount of business, the company should give him a trip or make some show of appreciation. Such recognition is a great way to motivate employees because at the heart of it, you're sharing your success. Other perks include insurance, dental, and medical expenses; expense accounts; and cars, which a lot of companies can write off as deductible expenses. A good pension plan is another form of recognition.

There's only one problem with perks: the IRS. Just before John Havlicek retired from the NBA, every league club gave him a gift at a ceremony during the last games he played at their home courts. John had all these wonderful remembrances, except that the IRS also knew about every one. Unfortunately, they watch TV, too.

Deferred Payments

I don't like deferred payments unless there is interest attached to them. If there is no interest—as with most deferred-payment plans—then it's best to take the money now and invest it yourself. But deferred payment—even without interest—*is* a good device to use if you're talking about a lot of money and you don't want it all today. Many people like to know they're going to see a certain amount of money for many years to come. A lot of ballplayers like deferred payments because they know they can count on the security of income coming in long after they're finished playing ball. It also keeps them emotionally attached to what they've been doing.

Committing Yourself to an Agreement

Verbal contracts mean nothing! Remember Aron Toder? We had an oral contract, but I got nothing when I went around to collect. Aron kept saying, "Not to worry," and kept stalling me, and I had no other choice because I wanted to learn the business. But if he wanted me, and it was the right opportunity for me, it should have been on paper. Don't work on promises. You'll get nothing that way.

If someone really wants you, if they need you, get the terms on paper.

Every agreement is a series of clauses, each conveying a specific item, such as salary, guarantee, bonuses, etc. You should write these clauses in draft form and give the contract to an attorney *who specializes in your field* so that he can go over it.

After I negotiate a contract, I like to send a telegram or a letter saying, "As per our conversation, the following has been agreed on . . ."; and then I list the items.

For instance, when I completed Ron Jackson's negotiation, it was two hours before the free-agency deadline. Had we gone over the allotted time, we would not have been able to negotiate with the Angels. Because time was of the essence, I sent a telegram to the Angels, and they sent one back confirming our agreement. And we were sure to send copies of our wires to the commissioner of baseball and to the baseball players association so that it was noted we had agreed.

During negotiations, arrangements can be made as to who will actually draw up a contract. Naturally, I prefer to be the one who draws it up, using my own terminology. I feel safer that way.

Telephone

The phone is the worst way to negotiate because you don't know what the other side is doing. But if you do have to negotiate by phone, be sure you have every point written down on paper and go through your list while you're talking.

When someone telephones *you*, you might be thinking of things like a previous call, an argument you had at home, a chat with your secretary. You're not in a good position to negotiate if your mind is elsewhere. In a sense, you're being taken by surprise and are not prepared or *mentally* set.

The answer? Call back! Many times I tell the other side, "Let me call you right back." It pays for me to make the extra long-distance call because it puts me in a more aggressive position. I'm psyched up. Now I have the advantage.

And always end your conversation by telling the other party you're sending them a letter confirming the points you have discussed and agreed upon.

Letters

Should you ever negotiate through letters? I don't like to, but sometimes there is no choice. A club will send me a proposal; I make changes and return the proposal to them. They make changes and send it back to me. This could go on for a long time.

Anyone who *wants* to negotiate via letters doesn't want to stand up to face-to-face negotiations. Perhaps they're afraid you'll get the better of them; perhaps they know they're in a weak bargaining position. Try to find out *why* they're bargaining via letter and use that information.

Use of the Media

The media are very tricky to use in negotiating. Stories can come out inaccurately. Misquotes are common, and the real issue can get thrown seriously out of joint.

When Don Klosterman was with the Rams, he wanted to negotiate through the media. George Young, GM of the New York Giants, hates to negotiate through the media. If there's a problem, he wants to go face-to-face and doesn't want the publicity for himself. George Steinbrenner, on the other hand, loves the media. I don't think it's only ego—for him, it's smart business. Whether it's good publicity or bad, it gets him and the Yankees in the headlines, and that sells tickets.

For myself, I prefer privacy. There are some things, especially while negotiations are ongoing, that should not be made public. On the other hand, media coverage does add a certain excitement to the game.

Once when I was involved with the Vince Ferragamo negotiations, I got a call from a local Los Angeles news station. I was informed there was a quote on the wire—Klosterman was saying, "David Fishof doesn't know what he's doing." The reporter asked me to comment.

I told him that Klosterman was being totally unreasonable in his negotiating position and that if he was saying that I didn't know what I was doing, I could say the same about him.

An article came out in a Los Angeles paper the next day with the line: "Agent says Klosterman doesn't know what he's doing." They had my quote but never included Klosterman's comment that had triggered my response. So, I was made out to look like the guy sounding off.

Winning at Negotiations

Everyone negotiates all the time. The key to coming out a winner is to recognize that you are in *negotiations*. Don't expect a miracle. Don't expect someone to give you what you want, just because you want it. Go in and bargain for it. Ask for what you deserve. Don't make excuses; don't be embarrassed about *bargaining*. How often have you heard or told yourself, "It's not worth it," or "Who needs the hassle"?

Let me tell you, it's always worth it! I've come to accept negotiations as a way of life. And you, too, are negotiating whether you are aware of it or not. *So why not be aware of it?* Learn the rules, the tricks of the trade; knowing how to negotiate gives you the power to be a winner. And after all, that's what we all want.